THE CRUCIFIED KING

Also in this series:

The Word for the World (John chapters 1 – 6)

The Controversial Christ (John chapters 7 – 14)

The Crucified King

Growing with John's Gospel

Book 3: John chapters 15 – 21

Stephen Gaukroger
with Simon Fox

Crossway Books
Leicester

CROSSWAY BOOKS
38 De Montfort Street, Leicester LE1 7GP, England

First published 1996

British Library Cataloguing in Publication Data
A catalogue record for this book is available from the British Library.

ISBN 1-85684-146-4

Typeset in Great Britain by Avocet Typeset, Brill, Aylesbury, Bucks

Printed in Great Britain for Crossway Books by Cox and Wyman Ltd, Reading, Berkshire

CONTENTS

Introduction   1

1. Branches of the vine   5

2. Chosen out of the world   20

3. A blueprint for prayer   33

4. Faith under pressure   50

5. Annas and Caiaphas   60

6. Jesus the King on trial   69

7. The ultimate choice   79

8. The crucified King   91

9. Jesus is alive!   104

10. Thomas and Peter   115

INTRODUCTION

John was one of the twelve disciples chosen by Jesus. So what we have in the Gospel of John is not an account written by some idle spectator who was not really involved in the events described. This gospel was not written by someone who turned up on the scene, rather like a journalist, asking people what happened and then reporting second-hand facts. John was actually there, seeing everything at first hand.

These days many people receive the teletext services on their televisions. It's remarkable how quickly the news stories are included on the news pages of Ceefax and Oracle. They enable you to keep right up to date with the news, twenty-four hours a day. But there is a small time-lag between the event happening and the report of it getting on to the teletext pages.

However, there is no time-lag at all in John's Gospel. It wasn't that someone told someone who told someone who told someone who told John. He was actually there! He was called by Jesus to be one of the original proclaimers of the gospel. This is an eye-witness account from someone who walked with Jesus, talked with him, sat down to evening meals with him and chatted over the events of the day with him. John would have said to Jesus, 'What were you doing with that blind man this morning?' And Jesus would have answered, 'Well, I healed him, and I did it like this ... And when I've gone and the Holy Spirit comes you will be able to do the same thing, and it will happen like this ... and like this ...'

We all know that Jesus had twelve disciples. But John was not just one of the Twelve: he was one of the Three. The Three were Peter, James and John, the closest friends of Jesus. He had realized that he couldn't share himself fully with as many as twelve, so he chose three men out of the twelve to be his intimate confidants. In effect he was saying to them, 'I am going to share my life with you even more deeply, intimately and fully than with those other nine. I am going to share with you my principles of living, my principles of power.'

Chapter 9 of Mark's Gospel tells the story of the Transfiguration, in which Jesus takes these three men up a mountain, where they have an amazing experience: the glory of God descends upon Jesus, his clothes become dazzling white, and they see him somehow talking with Elijah and Moses, two of the Old Testament prophets. Only these three disciples had the privilege of seeing that great event, and John was one of them.

And not only was John one of the Three, but he was also the disciple who was closest to Jesus. In John 13:23 we read that at the Last Supper John, *the disciple whom Jesus loved, was reclining next to him.* In the ancient world people didn't eat at a table, sitting on chairs. Instead they ate lying down in a circle, leaning on one elbow. So John would have been lying next to Jesus, and they would have been able to talk about things quietly and intimately while they were eating together. Jesus shared some very important truths with John, his close friend, and John wrote them down for us so that we too can know Jesus personally.

Mark's Gospel was the first of the four gospels to be written. It is short, pithy and to the point; it has no long explanations. It is full of action and life. Then Matthew's Gospel was written especially for the Jews who needed a lot of explanations about Jesus. They knew all about Yahweh, the great God of the Old Testament, but who was this Jesus person? Then there was Luke's Gospel, which was written for the Gentiles, who had never heard of either Yahweh or Jesus and who needed a factual account of Jesus' life. That's why the story of his birth is fuller in Luke than in any other gospel. Luke was explaining to the Gentiles who Jesus was and where he came from. John's Gospel was the last to be written (perhaps at around AD 80), and it was an attempt to say to the world, 'This is what Jesus means.' It is a gospel of explanation, a gospel of purpose. There are only eight miracles recorded in John, while there are dozens in the other gospels. John isolates each miracle and makes a point out of it and says, 'This is who Jesus is, this is why he came into the world.'

If you are not yet a Christian or have only recently become one, there is no better place to begin learning about Jesus than in John's Gospel. Even if you have been a Christian for decades, there are truths in this gospel which will amaze you.

Chapter 1

Branches of the vine

I am the true vine, and my Father is the gardener. He cuts off every branch in me that bears no fruit, while every branch that does bear fruit he prunes so that it will be even more fruitful. You are already clean because of the word I have spoken to you. Remain in me, and I will remain in you. No branch can bear fruit by itself; it must remain in the vine. Neither can you bear fruit unless you remain in me.

I am the vine; you are the branches. If a man remains in me and I in him, he will bear much fruit; apart from me you can do nothing.

(John 15:1–5)

Jesus the true vine

In his teaching, Jesus used pictures and symbols that the people of his time would have understood. So, for example, in this passage he talks about a vine, because that was an image which the people could have easily grasped. If Jesus were here in the flesh today, he might use rather different imagery. Because the culture of our day is so different from that of first-century Palestine, the significance of Jesus' picture-language is not as readily apparent to us as it would have been to those who first heard his teaching. In an industrialized country like Britain, few people have any knowledge or understanding about vines and vineyards, and we can appreciate the full meaning of what Jesus is saying only by doing some background reading. However, the spiritual truth which he was expressing through this teaching is as powerful today as when he first spoke it. In talking about the vine Jesus was talking about himself and what he said about himself then is still true today.

When the Jews heard Jesus speaking about a vine, they would have thought of it in a negative sense. In the Old Testament, and particularly in the books of Isaiah and Jeremiah, Israel is depicted as a vine which is rotten and out of control. The prophets were saying to the people, 'You're an overgrown vine – you have outgrown your usefulness. You destroy everything you touch, you crush things which are fragile; you are an ugly intruder.' The people of Israel obeyed God when they felt like it but ignored him or directly rebelled against him when it suited them. God was the Gardener of the vine, but the vine resisted his efforts to tame it. But Jesus was now saying to the Jews, *I am the true vine.* In other words, he was saying that, unlike Israel, he was a healthy, good vine, which was fully under the control of the Gardener. Jesus was always obedient to his Father.

Jesus told his disciples,

No branch can bear fruit by itself; it must remain in the vine. Neither can you bear fruit unless you remain in me.

(John 15:4)

Jesus was here using a very simple principle of gardening to illustrate a spiritual truth. If a branch is cut off from the rest of the plant, it rapidly withers and dies because it has been isolated from the plant's roots, which provide all of its nourishment. So an isolated branch cannot bear any fruit because it has no nourishment in it. Similarly, Christians need to be part of the spiritual vine which is Jesus. If an individual Christian detaches himself from a close walk with Jesus, he or she becomes spiritually dried up and incapable of bearing

6

the fruit of the Spirit. If we detach ourselves from Jesus, we will become useless to him. But if we remain in him, in close contact with him, in love with him, we will remain fertile, strong and fruitful, and our lives will be accomplishing something for God.

If we are Christians we are also members of the church. We cannot be Christians without being in the church. When Jesus ascended to heaven after his resurrection, he left behind the church to be his agent and representative on earth. The Bible calls the church 'the body of Christ'; it is Jesus' hands and feet to do his work on earth. If we try to distance ourselves from the church, we will also be distancing ourselves from Jesus; if we try to drop out of church involvement, we will also start to drop out of involvement with Jesus. In very exceptional circumstances Christians may remain close to Jesus while being isolated from the church; for example, if they are imprisoned for their faith and kept in solitary confinement. But such cases are very rare.

I'm sorry to say that I have known a lot of Christians who have drifted away from Jesus and his body, the church. At first they were walking with him and everything seemed to be going well in their lives. Then I could see that they had taken one step away from Jesus: in some way they had compromised their faith, or in some way they had found being a Christian too costly. Having taken the first step, they then took another, and another, until they were far from Jesus and spiritually shrivelled up. These people, who had once possessed a vibrant, joyful Christian faith, had become spiritually sterile and ineffective.

The celebrated English poet John Donne wrote, 'No man is an Island, entire of it self; every man is a piece of the Continent, a part of the main.' Donne was a very perceptive writer, and in this poem he was saying that no-one can exist in isolation; everyone is part of the 'Continent' which is the human race. That is true of

7

people in general, and it is even more true of Christians and the church. No Christian can survive as an island. We all need to be part of the mainland which is the body of Christ if we are to continue to thrive and flourish spiritually. To use another analogy, if someone's hand is chopped off, it cannot continue to live and function; it will soon die, because it has been isolated from the life-blood of the body and from the mind which controls the body. Similarly, if we are cut off from the body of Christ we will wither and die, because we will no longer have that body's life flowing through us.

Many years ago, in the days when every house had a coal fire, a minister was visiting some of his parishioners. He went to see one man who had not been to church for years. When the minister asked the man about this he replied, 'But I don't need to go to church. I pray and read the Bible on my own.'

The minister reached for a pair of tongs and drew a glowing coal out of the fire and set it down on the fireplace. As the conversation continued the coal glowed less and less and finally ceased to glow altogether. The minister then used this to illustrate the fact that however glowing our personal walk with God may be, if we remove ourselves from the spiritual fire which is the fellowship of other Christians we will eventually lose that glow and become cold and dead.

What is more, if we are isolated we will miss out on what God is doing in our generation. Generally, God works through his church, not through unsupported, isolated individuals. If we are out on the fringes of the church we will be mere spectators rather than participants in what God is doing.

The Divine Surgeon

Jesus said that God

... cuts off every branch in me that bears no fruit, while every branch that does bear fruit he prunes so that it will be even more fruitful.

(John 15:2)

God is a wise gardener, and so he knows that pruning, while it looks like a vicious, harmful thing to do, actually enables the plant to produce better and more fruit.

When I was a teenager living with my parents in Preston, an elderly lady whom we knew asked me if I wouldn't mind pruning the roses in her garden, as she no longer had the strength for it. I agreed to do it, but since I didn't know anything about roses I looked the subject up in a few gardening books. Armed with this knowledge, I went to the lady's garden to tidy up her roses for her. I started off using a small pair of secateurs, but since this proved to be too laborious, I set to work with an enormous pair of garden shears which I had brought. In my ignorance I severely hacked the rose-bushes so that they were only about nine inches tall! The lady came out and was very pleased, as the bushes certainly looked much tidier, even though they had been massacred. Amazingly, the bushes survived my savage attack and that year produced the best roses they had grown for a long time. This just goes to show that even a complete amateur can make plants grow better with a bit of pruning.

There are sinful things in the lives of all Christians which God wants to prune away. The pruning is inevitably painful, but it is well worth it. God is no amateur, so when he prunes us the result is a dramatic improvement in our fruit-bearing ability. When he prunes us, he does not come at us with a huge pair of shears, as I did with those unfortunate roses. God is not an axe-man, an indiscriminate hacker, an insensitive bludgeoner. When I chopped away at those rose-bushes I didn't know what I was doing, but God knows precisely what he is doing when he prunes us. To use another metaphor, God is an expert diamond-cutter who cuts away at the raw stone to produce a gem which expresses the beauty of his Son. He carefully hones and polishes the original stone until he has produced something wonderful. He is a skilled craftsman who works meticulously to make our lives beautiful for his glory.

When we feel pain, it will often be because God is pruning us. Often God will use painful and difficult circumstances to prune us. We may go through a severe trial or crisis, and through it God changes us so that we more closely resemble Jesus. C. S. Lewis wisely said, 'God whispers to us in our pleasures but shouts to us in our pain. It is his megaphone to rouse a deaf world.' I know that I certainly need to change a lot; there are all sorts of ways in which I need to become more Christ-like, and that transformation will happen through the pains and stresses in my life.

All Christians must experience this pain of pruning, and we also need to understand what God is doing through it. If we are suffering, it does not mean that God has abandoned us; it means he is pruning us. If we don't recognize this need for pruning we will become confused by the suffering. We will feel angry with God, with other Christians and with ourselves.

Part of being a Christian is this willingness to submit to the Gardener's pruning. Real Christianity is not just some sort of vague lifestyle in which we all carry on being much as we were before we were converted. It is a willingness to let the Divine Surgeon carry out the surgery which we so desperately need.

If we ask God to make us more Christlike, we should not pray that prayer superficially, because when God answers it there is bound to be some pruning involved. Becoming more like Jesus is costly. The Bible says it is an awful thing to fall into the hands of the living God, and it certainly is. We need to understand the consequences of asking God to make us Christlike.

When God prunes us we usually try to resist it. Often that pruning will cut across the grain of our pride and ego and sense of achievement, and so we try to dodge the painful process. But if we sincerely want to bear more fruit for God, we must open to his pruning. Of course, in one sense we are not like the vine branches in Jesus' word-picture here in John 15. Actual vines are passive and have no choice when the gardener comes to prune them. But we do have a choice. We can shy away from God's secateurs. God will not prune us against our will. If we refuse to allow him to prune us through our pain, he will respect that choice. The pain will simply be pain, without any productive purpose. He says to us, 'I want you to be willing to be made like the Lord Jesus.' When the Divine Surgeon comes to us with his knife to cut out the sinful growths in our lives, we must willingly consent, because without that willingness he will not operate, and if he does not operate we will not get better.

Most of us want all the gifts which God wants to give us, but we don't want the pruning and the discipline which we also need. We will gladly accept any material gift, such as a new job or some unexpected money. We are eager for spiritual gifts and for the fruit of the Spirit. We will gladly take all the peace, joy and love which God cares to give us. But when God says to us, 'My beloved child, there is a part of your life which is wrong and needs to be removed. Please let me operate on it,' we draw back. That is not the sort of gift we want from our Father! We don't want God to deal with our bad temper or our sexual promiscuity or our material greed or our gossiping tongue or our lying or our manipulation of other people. We like all these things and we don't want God to take them away. But once we submit to God's knife, we will bear far more spiritual fruit.

Do we want to be fruitful? Do we want to glorify and honour God? Do we want to be filled with the fruit of the Spirit? Do we want people to become converted through our Christian witness? Of course we do, but there is no easy way to get these things. We have to be willing to be pruned by God.

Depending on Jesus

Jesus said, *apart from me you can do nothing* (John 15:5). But in practice most Christians don't believe this. We believe that apart from God we can be superbly well organized and really enthusiastic, that apart from him we can achieve real progress in our work as churches and we can set up lots of successful projects, and if Jesus blesses our activities and efforts, so much the better. Often that is the thinking which underlies much of our church life. But this idea is false, because the truth is that without Jesus we can achieve nothing of lasting value. We may be able to accomplish many things in our own strength, but they will not be permanent achievements. For example, having a large number of people in church on Sunday morning is not necessarily a sign of true spiritual success. The question is: why are they there, and will they keep coming and commit their lives to Jesus? We could attract a lot of people to church by offering to give them money if they will turn up, but there would be no real achievement in that! Real success is measured by what the Holy Spirit is doing among those people. We cannot manufacture a revival by ourselves; we have to depend upon Jesus to do it for us and through us. Without him we can do nothing of permanent significance. That is a truth which needs to infiltrate every level and every area of our church life.

Jesus said:

My command is this: Love each other as I have loved you.

(verse 12)

We need to remember that Jesus has *commanded* us to love one another. It is not an optional extra, it is not something we have a choice about, it is not something we start to do once we have become spiritually mature. It is what the life of the church is all about. Jesus did not command us to *like* one another. Liking is an emotional response, and we cannot make ourselves like people we would not naturally like. But loving one another is not to do with our emotions but to do with our wills. We love one another by our actions, by *doing* loving things to one another.

There is an amazing consequence to our loving one another:

You are my friends if you do what I command [that is, to love one another]. *I no longer call you servants, because a servant does not know his master's business. Instead, I have called you friends.*

(verses 14–15)

It is astonishing to think that every Christian can be a friend of Jesus. Jesus is God, and therefore he is all-knowing and all-powerful. Yet if we love one another we can be his friends and he will be our friend.

One of the characteristics of friendship is sharing one's thoughts with one's friend. Often when I pray I find myself thinking most about how great and powerful God is and how insignificant I am compared with him, and yet sometimes I can feel the friendship which exists between Jesus and me. I sense him sharing his thoughts with me, and I share my thoughts with him. Since I am his friend, he wants to let me in on his plans. I am not a mere servant who simply has to do what he is told without understanding anything of the

Master's overall plan. Because of my friendship relationship with him I can ask him, 'Lord, what are your plans for me? What do you want to do in this church? What have you got in mind for this town? What are you saying to this nation?'

Sometimes I will even ask the daring question, 'Lord, what do you think about me? Does the way I am living please you?' Then I might get a positive answer, or the Lord might point out a few areas where I need to change! That is the mark of a real friend as opposed to a mere acquaintance. Real friends care about you so much that they are prepared to be honest with you about yourself, even though they know you won't like it!

I have a friend whom I have known since we went to Spurgeon's College together, and he knows me so well that sometimes he will be frank with me and will put me right about one or two things. I am grateful to have a friend like that, and I am glad that Jesus is that sort of friend too. He is not the sort of friend who will always agree with you just to keep the relationship ticking over without any tensions or conflict. Real friends know they can disagree with you and still be your friends, because your friendship is strong enough to take that conflict. Jesus is prepared to tell us the truth about ourselves not *despite* our friendship but *because* he is our friend. He tells us the truth because he loves us and cares about us.

Some Christians, however, have never sat down in the presence of Jesus long enough to ask him what he thinks of them. Or if he has told them, they have ignored it because they didn't like what they were hearing. We all need to ask Jesus, 'Lord, what do you think of our friendship? Are you glad to have me as a friend? Is there anything about me that you would like to change? What kind of friendship do you want with me? What are you getting out of our friendship?'

He will answer questions like that, and if we listen

14

and obey we will become more like the kind of friends Jesus wants us to be.

Lasting fruit

Jesus told the disciples,

You did not choose me, but I chose you and appointed you to go and bear fruit – fruit that will last.

(John 15:16)

Jesus had chosen the disciples to be his apostles, the founders of his church, which was to last from the time of Acts until the present day, and which will continue until Jesus returns. Jesus wanted the disciples to remain in him, depending on him for everything, so that they would bear lasting fruit. They would be able to do things in the world which would be of permanent significance.

Today we live in a world which is changing very rapidly. We see new technologies changing our daily lives; at our places of work we see people being replaced by computers. We see rapid change in the national scene; we had the boom of the mid-eighties and the deep recession of the late eighties and early nineties. We see the map of the world being transformed at an astonishing rate. The Soviet Union has collapsed, introducing new freedom but also new instability into the world. We see Europe rushing headlong towards a federal future. We see the global environment changing in a highly disturbing manner; the climate in northern Europe is getting hotter, while vast, dangerous holes have appeared in the ozone layer over the two poles. In today's world nothing seems to be permanent, and it seems to be anyone's guess what the future will bring. But as Christians, as people of the kingdom of God, we can work for things which will have permanent value and importance, no matter what else happens in the world.

Jesus want us to bear fruit that will last. This means that we have to be *committed to permanence.* In our individual lives and in our churches we need to be working to create a permanent transformation in the community around us. What is needed is not just a brief outpouring of God's power, which creates a stir in the church and sends out short-lived ripples into the community, but the building of spiritual structures which stand the test of time and will go on glorifying God permanently. We want people's lives to be changed and to stay changed. Our churches need to be revolutionary, but in a permanent sense. Our own lives need to be permanently changed so that we become more Christlike and go on changing into Jesus' likeness. This will convince the people around us that God is truly alive today.

We need to take the long-term view of things, as God does. The way we live our Christian lives today can have repercussions for generations after our own time. For example, through our witness a neighbour may become a Christian. As a result of that, his or her spouse gets converted, and then together they teach their children about Jesus. Eventually those children become committed Christians, and they go on to find Christian marriage partners, and then they too have children and teach them about the Lord. And so it can go on, for generation after generation. As a result of one person being saved, an entire family gets converted. Their Christian witness spills over into other families, and so entire communities are touched by the power of God. We don't know when Jesus is going to return, but when he does, the work we have done for his kingdom in our own lifetimes will still be bearing fruit then, no matter how many generations later it may be. We may have died long ago, but we will have built something of lasting, eternal value.

Friends of Jesus

On one occasion an expert in the Jewish religious law had asked Jesus which was the most important of the commandments which God had given to his people. Jesus replied by quoting two commandments from the Old Testament:

'Love the Lord your God with all your heart and with all your soul and with all your mind.' This is the first and greatest commandment. And the second is like it: 'Love your neighbour as yourself.' All the Law and the Prophets hang on these two commandments.

(Matthew 22:37–40)

The whole of the duty of God's people could be summed up in these two commandments to love God and one's neighbour.

And now in John's Gospel Jesus gives an additional commandment to his disciples:

My command is this: Love each other as I have loved you.

(John 15:12)

By his way of life, Jesus had been a living demonstration to the disciples of what it really meant to love one's neighbour as oneself, and so what he wanted them to do was to follow his example. Just as he had loved them, he wanted them to love one another. This was to be more important than they then realized, because before very long Jesus would no longer be with them. To live as he wanted them to live, they would have to remember how he had lived and seek to emulate him.

The supreme expression of Jesus' love for them was yet to come.

Greater love has no-one than this, that he lay down his life for his friends.

(verse 13)

The disciples probably didn't understand it at the time, but Jesus was literally going to lay down his life for them, his friends. He was going to allow himself to be crucified as the sacrifice to cleanse them (and all people) from their sins. Jesus was going to lay down his life for others in a way that no-one else in all history had ever done before or would ever be able to do again, for he was the only Son of God. He was the only one who could be the sacrifice for humankind's sins, and once he had made that sacrifice, there would never need to be another.

And yet Jesus was also calling his disciples to lay down their lives for one another. This applied to the Twelve and also to all disciples of Jesus in all ages. How can we lay down our lives for our friends? By living to serve them, by living lives of Christlike love. And in some cases Christians are called to give up their lives for their brothers and sisters in a very literal sense. Through the centuries of persecution, there have been many Christians who have given up their lives to protect their fellow believers. The present century has seen some of the most savage persecution of Christians in the history of the church, especially in Communist and Islamic countries. We will never know (until Jesus returns) how many Christians have died under torture rather than give their torturers the names of their Christian brethren. They gave up their lives for their friends.

Jesus then said,

You are my friends if you do what I command. I no longer call you servants, because a servant does not know his master's business. Instead, I have called you friends, for everything that I learned from my Father I have made known to you.

(John 15:14–15)

What a tremendous privilege it was for the disciples to be called friends by Jesus! They were not mere servants. He had shared the secrets of his Father with them, he had shared his gospel with them, he had shared with them the longings and desires and burdens of his heart as the Messiah. But there was a condition attached to this very special friendship. Jesus would share his heart of hearts only with those who obeyed him.

Just as the disciples were Jesus' friends, so too are we, and the same condition applies to us. If we choose to obey him and follow him as our Lord, we will be more than mere servants to him. We will be his friends. He will share with us the secrets of his heart. When we pray to him he will talk to us in the heart-to-heart way that friends talk. He will share with us the concerns and burdens on his heart. He will share his feelings with us, he will make us care about the things and people he cares about, he will make our hearts beat in time with his own heart. This is what it means to be a friend of Jesus, and it is the greatest privilege and honour that anyone can ever know.

Chapter 2

Chosen out of the world

> *If the world hates you, keep in mind that it hated me first.*
> *If you belonged to the world, it would love you as its own.*
> *As it is, you do not belong to the world, but I have chosen*
> *you out of the world. That is why the world hates you.*
>
> (John 15:18–19)

Why does the world hate Christians? Quite simply because we are not of the world. Jesus said, *I have chosen you out of the world* (verse 19). We are still in the world, but we do not belong to it. *If you belonged to the world, it would love you as its own* (verse 19). Instead we belong not to the world but to Jesus. Just by being Christians, we are an accusation against the world and its sinfulness. The devil, the prince of this world, hates us because in becoming Christians we have been removed from his control and enlisted into God's army to fight against the devil. The world hates us because we are God's soldiers and servants. Jesus warns us that if we work and fight in his name, we will be persecuted:

If they persecuted me, they will persecute you also ... They will treat you this way because of my name.

> (verses 20–21)

Right from the start, Jesus' ministry tended to divide people into two groups: those who welcomed him and his message gladly, and those who rejected him. The powerful people in the society in which he lived – the Jewish political and religious leaders – rejected and opposed him, because they knew that his gospel teaching and popularity among the poor people were undermining their power in the nation.

Jesus knew what it was like to be hated and opposed by the world, so when we are on the receiving end of opposition or persecution or discrimination because we are Christians, when we feel we are hated by the world, we should remember that we are in excellent company. Jesus told the disciples:

No servant is greater than his master.

(verse 20)

So if the Master was hated and persecuted by the world, then his servants should expect the same treatment. If we are sincerely trying to be disciples of Jesus and to follow in his footsteps, then we will surely encounter opposition and hatred.

Persecution

For most of us living in the Western world at the present time, that opposition is fairly mild compared to what Christians in other centuries had to endure. The Christians in the early years of the church experienced ruthless persecution at the hands of some of the Roman emperors. The most infamous of them was Nero, who entertained the mobs of Rome by feeding Christians to the lions in the Colosseum and using them as human torches to illuminate the gardens of his palace during night-time parties.

In Britain too, Christians have at various times suffered persecution. During the reigns of Henry VIII and Queen Mary in the sixteenth century, Christians who wanted to practise a biblically based faith were at times severely punished. Queen Mary was given the nickname 'Bloody Mary' because she put Bible-believing Christians to death.

And, as we saw in chapter 1, in modern times in

some parts of the world, Christians have been killed for their faith. In Communist Eastern Europe and the USSR, generations of Christians experienced the most bitter and savage persecution. Vast numbers of them were incarcerated for their faith and many thousands of them died in prison camps. Thankfully, with the recent collapse of Communism in Europe and Russia, the persecution of Christians there has been greatly reduced.

However, persecution is by no means a thing of the past. In some Muslim countries today it is illegal for Muslims to become Christians, and those who do so receive brutal treatment. Also we should not forget that China, with its one billion or more people (a quarter of the human race), is still a one-party state in which any criticism of the government is forcefully suppressed (as the brave young students at Tiananmen Square in Beijing discovered to their cost). It is not illegal to be a Christian in China, but it is certainly interpreted as opposition to the government. Anyone in China who preaches the gospel boldly and publicly is likely to end up in trouble.

Compared with all this, the persecution which we suffer is mild. However, it can still be very unpleasant. For example, we may be ridiculed for our faith. A teenager at school who gives his life to Jesus will probably have to endure some teasing. His peers may be annoyed by the stand he has taken. In effect the young Christian has said to the other students, 'I don't like the way you're living. It's not for me. I'm opting for something much better. I'm going to live for Jesus.'

Or people may find that their Christian commitment provokes a hostile response at work. They might not talk a lot about their faith, but their unwillingness to tell or listen to smutty jokes in the factory canteen, or their reluctance to get involved in bitching and back-biting in the office, may irritate their workmates. The

Christians' refusal to say and do the negative things which everyone else is saying and doing is perceived as a haughty, 'holier-than-thou' attitude. In some situations just being a Christian makes us stand out like a sore thumb.

Sometimes even in our 'tolerant' society, persecution may become blatant, and Christians may even find themselves being subjected to physical violence. For example, a couple of years ago an evangelist shared the gospel message with a group of teenagers on the London Underground. Apparently they didn't like what he said, because they beat him up afterwards. Fortunately, he was a physically strong man from a very tough background, so he knew how to protect himself from serious harm. But it was hard for him to just stand there while these teenagers went on and on pumelling him. He was quite capable of knocking all of them to the floor, but he managed to resist the temptation!

Whatever form it takes, persecution hurts. So we need to make these words of the apostle Paul our motto:

We are hard pressed on every side, but not crushed; perplexed, but not in despair; persecuted, but not abandoned; struck down, but not destroyed.

(2 Corinthians 4:8–9)

We need to remember that we are hated by a world which has been conquered by Jesus, so in the last analysis we don't need to fear the world's hatred. We have been saved eternally by Jesus, so there is a limit to the harm which the world can do to us. This is a world of death, but Jesus has delivered us from death and brought us into life. We are in the world, but we do not belong to it.

A gospel which offends

It is part of the church's witness that we should be

concerned about the needy and vulnerable people in our communities. But there should be more to our witness than that; we must also preach the gospel. If all that Christians did was to show social concern, the world would love us; they would not be offended by us. But when Christians preach the gospel message that all people are sinners, and that they need to turn to Jesus to be saved from their sins, people get upset. People don't like being told that they are sinners in rebellion against God. It makes them angry when we tell them that Jesus died on the cross because of their sins, that his blood was shed to cleanse them from their wickedness, and they have no hope of going to heaven without accepting him as their Saviour. Yes, the gospel message is all about God's love for us, but the sting of the message is that God loves us *even though we are sinners,* and that he sent Jesus to die for us so that we could be forgiven. People like to hear about God's love for them, but they don't like to hear about their own selfishness.

We need to understand clearly that the gospel message is always going to offend people. Just like children when they have been naughty, people don't like being told off! They don't like having their sinfulness pointed out to them. Whenever the gospel of Jesus is faithfully and clearly preached, it always divides people. There will be some who will say in their hearts, 'I know that's true. I must turn to Jesus.' There will be others who will say in their hearts, 'I know that's true. I don't want to hear it.' And if people don't want to hear the gospel message, they will sometimes take steps to silence the person who is delivering it.

Jesus said:

If I had not come and spoken to them, they would not be guilty of sin. Now, however, they have no excuse for their sin.

(John 15:22)

24

Jesus had come to the Jews of his time and had preached the good news to them, but they had rejected it.

If I had not done among them what no-one else did, they would not be guilty of sin. But now they have seen these miracles, and yet they have hated both me and my Father.

(verse 24)

Jesus had come to them and done many miracles, and so there could be no doubt that he possessed the power of God as no-one else had ever done before. It was plain for all to see that he was the Son of God, and yet they still refused to believe in him. They had rejected both Jesus' words and Jesus' works, and so they were now doubly guilty of the sin of rejecting him.

This was true of the people of Jesus' own time, and it is still true of people today. The gospel of Jesus Christ is being preached today, and miracles of God's power are happening today. Some people are convinced by the message and the miracle and turn to Jesus, but there are others who scoff and turn away. They know in their heart of hearts that Jesus is the Saviour, but they refuse to acknowledge him. We should be prepared for this. There will always be some people who respond to the gospel message, and others who reject it. This is nothing new. There were those who rejected Jesus in his own lifetime, and there are those who reject him today. And because they reject and hate him, they reject and hate those who have accepted him.

The promise of the Spirit

After hearing all these dire warnings about the hatred of the world, the disciples must have been asking themselves how they would survive as followers of Jesus. To encourage them he reminded them of the promise about the Holy Spirit which he had already made:

When the Counsellor comes, whom I will send to you from the Father, the Spirit of truth who goes out from the Father, he will testify about me.

(John 15:26)

After he had ascended to heaven, Jesus was going to send the Holy Spirit to the disciples (Acts 2 records this event). So the disciples would not be left alone after Jesus had gone. They would have his Holy Spirit with them.

Jesus was going to ascend to heaven, and so he would not be physically present on earth any more. And yet he would still be with his disciples in the person of the Holy Spirit. The Spirit would reveal Jesus to the people of God; they would see Jesus, even though he was in heaven. And the same is still true for us today: the Holy Spirit reveals Jesus to us. It is by the Holy Spirit that we know Jesus.

In John 14:26 Jesus had told the disciples,

... the Counsellor, the Holy Spirit, whom the Father will send in my name, will teach you all things and will remind you of everything I have said to you.

Jesus' teaching ministry would end with his ascension, but the Holy Spirit would continue it, reaffirming everything Jesus had told his disciples. And today it is the Holy Spirit who teaches us through the words of Scripture and also through words of prophecy: by the Holy Spirit Jesus is still speaking to us and teaching us today.

Jesus said that the Holy Spirit would *testify about me* (John 15:26). It is the Holy Spirit who speaks to people's hearts about Jesus and brings them to conversion as they put their trust in him as their Saviour. The Holy Spirit testifies to our hearts about Jesus.

Jesus told the disciples,

I tell you the truth: It is for your good that I am going away.
(John 16:7)

He was going to ascend to heaven, and he was saying that this was for the disciples' good. How could this be? What did he mean? In the same verse he explained:

Unless I go away, the Counsellor will not come to you; but if I go, I will send him to you.

The Holy Spirit would not be sent until Jesus had gone to be with the Father.

When he said that it was for the disciples' good that he went away, Jesus meant that through his Holy Spirit he would be able to work much more widely in the world. As a human being Jesus had voluntarily limited himself. He could be at only one place at any given time. But once he had ascended to heaven and the Holy Spirit had been sent on the church, Jesus was able to work through the Spirit all over the world, in any number of places.

And that is what he has done throughout the history of the church up to the present day. He has been working simultaneously all over the world in any number of places at any given time.

Jesus said,

When he, the Spirit of truth, comes, he will guide you into all truth. He will not speak on his own; he will speak only what he hears, and he will tell you what is yet to come. He will bring glory to me by taking from what is mine and making it known to you. All that belongs to the Father is mine.

(John 16:13–15)

We see all three Persons of the Trinity here: the Father, Jesus, and the Holy Spirit. First, *All that belongs to the Father is mine.* Jesus is the Son of God, and so he shares in everything that belongs to the Father. And then the Holy Spirit brings glory to Jesus by taking from what belongs to Jesus and making it known to the people of God. Do you see the two steps in that? Jesus receives from the Father, and the Spirit passes on the blessings from Jesus to us.

In a nutshell, then, the Spirit's role is to make Jesus known to us, to bring glory to Jesus, to make Jesus real to us. *He will bring glory to me by taking from what is mine and making it known to you.*

An optional extra?

There is a tendency for Christians to think that the Holy Spirit is some kind of optional extra for 'super-spiritual' Christians only. But that isn't what Scripture tells us. Scripture shows us that everything about us Christians is done by and through the Holy Spirit.

Who is it who brings us to the point where we put our faith in Jesus as our Saviour? It's the Holy Spirit. Who is it who makes us born again in Jesus Christ? It's the Holy Spirit. Who is it who comes and lives in us once we are converted? The Holy Spirit. Who is it who enables us to know Jesus and to have a personal relationship with him? The Holy Spirit. Who is it who gives us the spiritual power to live as Christians and to glorify Jesus in our lives? The Holy Spirit. Who is it who enables us to exercise faith and to pray to God and to worship God? The Holy Spirit. Who is it who heals us when we pray for healing? The Holy Spirit. Who is it who progressively changes us so that we increasingly resemble Jesus? The Holy Spirit does that.

The Holy Spirit affects our lives not only when we ask to be filled with the Holy Spirit. The Holy Spirit is the one who enables us to do all the things which are part and parcel of just being a Christian. Without the Holy Spirit, no-one could be a Christian, no-one could know Jesus at all (Romans 8:9).

The Holy Spirit is not an optional extra in the Christian life. The Christian life is a relationship with

Jesus, but it is also a relationship with the Holy Spirit. Everything that we are and do as Christians, we are and do through the Holy Spirit, in the power of the Holy Spirit.

Normally we talk about our Christian faith as a relationship with Jesus, and this is perfectly right and proper, because it is the Holy Spirit's role to glorify Jesus, and to uplift the name of Jesus. Jesus is meant to be the focus of our faith. As Christians we are involved in a love relationship with Jesus, and everything in that relationship happens and is made possible by and through the Holy Spirit.

So the role of the Holy Spirit is to make Jesus real to us – not just in being saved from our sins at our conversion, but throughout our lives as Christians, right until the day our bodies die and we pass on into God's glory. Jesus is in heaven with the Father, but through the Holy Spirit Jesus is also here on earth with us today. Jesus is Immanuel, 'God with us'.

Fruit and power

One way of describing the way we grow more mature as Christians is that Jesus becomes more and more real to us. Jesus wants to make himself real to us not just when we are converted, but all the time, in ever-increasing measure. Jesus wants us to know him in ever-increasing reality. I think there are two aspects to this.

First, Jesus wants to make himself more real to us in *transforming* us so that we increasingly resemble him, so that we are people who are always becoming more Christlike, full of his love and goodness. Really we are talking here about the fruit of the Spirit:

love, joy, peace, patience, kindness, goodness, faithfulness, gentleness and self-control.

(Galatians 5:22–23)

Jesus makes us produce this fruit in our lives by the Holy Spirit.

And secondly, Jesus wants to make himself more real to us in terms of his power. Jesus wants to fill us with his power so that we can serve and glorify him in the world and be a blessing to the people around us. Jesus wants us to have his power in our lives. All of the power which Jesus gives us is the power of his Holy Spirit. Here we're thinking about being filled with the Spirit. We are talking about the gifts of the Spirit rather than the fruit of the Spirit.

Jesus does both of these things through the Holy Spirit: causing us to bear the fruit of the Holy Spirit in our lives and empowering us with the Holy Spirit and his gifts. These are the two aspects of the work which the Holy Spirit does in us. They are two sides of a coin, but it is only one coin. There is only one Holy Spirit, and the work which he does is a single, unified, integrated work. The Holy Spirit who, for example, enables us to be self-controlled is the same Holy Spirit who gives gifts of tongues, prophecy, healing and so on.

We need not only to display the fruit of the Spirit in our lives; we also need the enabling of the Spirit. We not only need God's love and goodness in us, but we also need the power to communicate that goodness and love to other people.

Equally, just having the power of the Spirit is of limited use if we don't also have the fruit of the Spirit. Someone may have a spectacular spiritual gift, but its effectiveness will be limited if that person is not also someone who radiates God's love, goodness and humility. It is tragic when a person's spiritual gift is nullified by a lack of Christlikeness in his or her life.

The Holy Spirit's role is to make Jesus Christ real in our lives. We receive the Holy Spirit when we become Christians, but we need to keep on receiving him throughout our Christian lives, so that Jesus becomes ever more real to us, so that the life of Jesus in us is growing ever more powerful. To that end we frequently need to ask Jesus to fill us with his Holy Spirit, and we will also find it helpful to have other people to pray that prayer for us.

Perhaps you want Jesus to be more real to you; you want more power from God to serve him. Perhaps Jesus felt very real to you at some time in the past, but more recently you haven't felt his presence very much, and you want to feel his presence with you again. Or perhaps you just want more of God's power so that you can serve him and bless other people more effectively. Jesus said:

Ask and it will be given to you; seek and you will find; knock and the door will be opened to you. For everyone who asks receives; he who seeks finds; and to him who knocks, the door will be opened.

Which of you fathers, if your son asks for fish, will give him a snake instead? Or if he asks for an egg, will give him a scorpion? If you, then, though you are evil, know how to give good gifts to your children, how much more will your Father in heaven give the Holy Spirit to those who ask him!

(Luke 11:9–13)

Expect trouble

Some Christians seem to believe that Jesus promised that being a Christian was going to be easy. But he never said any such thing. Indeed, he warned the disciples that they should expect the Christian life to be difficult and demanding. He said that if someone wanted to follow him, that person had to

… deny himself and take up his cross daily and follow me.

(Luke 9:23)

And he plainly told his disciples,

In this world you will have trouble.

(John 16:33; see also verse 20)

Nowhere in his teaching did Jesus promise his followers an easy ride. Being a Christian is a costly business.

But thankfully there is another side to this equation. Christianity is not all suffering and pain! Having told the disciples that *In this world you will have trouble*, he immediately reassured them by saying,

But take heart! I have overcome the world.

He was soon going to be crucified, but the disciples' grief would turn to joy when they met with their resurrected Lord. Today, we too can know and experience the risen Jesus. Just as he turned those first disciples' despair into a joy and power that would take the whole world by storm, so we can know Jesus' ability to overcome death, sin and all the evils of the world.

Whatever problems life may throw at us, in Jesus Christ, the One who has overcome the world, we have all the resources we need to cope with them – more than that, to overcome them! The apostle Paul found this to be true in his own life. When he was facing a particularly difficult problem, he asked Jesus three times to take it away. But Jesus said to him,

My grace is sufficient for you, for my power is made perfect in weakness.

(2 Corinthians 19:9)

Paul found that Jesus gave him all the grace and power he needed to cope with the situation he was facing.

But as well as giving us his strength here and now, Jesus also gives us a wonderful hope for the future. One day we are going to be living in heaven with Jesus, and today's problems will then pale into insignificance. The suffering we are enduring now may be severe, but one day we will forget all about it. There may be shadows in our lives now, but the joyful light of God's eternity will drive them away.

Chapter 3

A blueprint for prayer

Jesus ... looked towards heaven and prayed:
'Father, the time has come. Glorify your Son, that your
Son may glorify you. For you granted him authority over
all people that he might give eternal life to all those you
have given him. Now this is eternal life: that they may
know you, the only true God, and Jesus Christ, whom you
have sent. I have brought you glory on earth by
completing the work you gave me to do. And now, Father,
glorify me in your presence with the glory I had with you
before the world began.'

(John 17:1–5)

The whole of John 17 is taken up with a single prayer
offered by Jesus. It is often referred to as Jesus' High-
Priestly Prayer or Consecration Prayer. The four
Gospels contain quite a number of the prayers which
Jesus prayed in the hearing of other people, but nearly
all of them are remarkably brief. They were to the
point and incisive. For example, when Jesus raised
Lazarus from the dead he prayed aloud for the benefit
of those who were witnessing the event. But it was a very
short, simple prayer. Even the Lord's Prayer, which
Jesus gave to us as a model for the way we should pray,
is very brief. But it is crammed with important things,
and says to God just about everything we need to say to
him.

In a church which my family attended when I was a
child, the prayers on a Sunday morning were regularly

at least thirty minutes long! I used to fall asleep after a few minutes and then, when I woke up again, the person was still praying! Children couldn't concentrate on such lengthy prayers, and I suspect that most of the adults couldn't either, and during the half-hour-long prayers their minds probably wandered all over the place.

The length of the prayers we pray, then, is not a measure of our spirituality. In fact, Jesus condemned the Pharisees for praying long public prayers in order to give people the impression that they were devout. It is a good rule to pray long prayers in private and brief prayers in public. The only time when a long prayer is of spiritual value is when we are praying in private, when we are spending time alone with God, trying to find out what his will is and to know what his thoughts are.

Jesus was able to pray short, powerful prayers in public because he prayed so much in private; he had a very strong relationship with his Father. Often he would go off alone, getting away from his disciples and the crowds of followers, and would spend time with God, seeking his face. His public prayer was incisive and effective because it was supported by a great deal of private prayer. I think the reason some Christians pray at such length in public is that their private prayer lives are so inadequate.

Praying with your body

Jesus' High-Priestly Prayer here in John 17 has a number of lessons to teach us. In chapter 16 Jesus had been teaching the disciples about what was soon going to happen, and now *he looked towards heaven and prayed* (John 17:1). That little phrase is significant because it tells us something about the way in which Jesus prayed. By lifting his eyes towards heaven he was expressing the attitude of his heart – that is, he was approaching God with sincerity and humility. It was a symbolic action. The disciples, being Jews, would have understood this. What the Jews did with their bodies when they were praying was quite important to them. Often they would pray standing, sometimes on their knees, and sometimes prostrate on the ground. We never read of them sitting on chairs in the sort of crouched position which is so common in our modern evangelical churches!

The physical position which we adopt when we pray can sometimes be important. Usually we pray sitting down, and we pray in a semi-conversational way. There is nothing wrong with that; Jesus has told us that he is our friend and that we can talk to him as a friend. But sometimes, as the Holy Spirit prompts us, we need to show the attitude of our hearts by some physical expression. For example, if we are thanking and praising God for something we might want to stand up or even jump up and down! If we are concerned about something and are earnestly trying to find out what God wants us to do in some situation, it might be right for us to pray kneeling down. If we are very sorry about something and we want to express our remorse to God, we might lie down on the floor as a sign that we are humbling ourselves before him and asking for his forgiveness.

This may sound a little strange to some people, but there is a sound principle behind it. We are not just spirits: we are mind-body-spirits. Our body is part of who we are, and by it we express what is going on in our spirit. If our spirit is rejoicing or concerned or repentant, expressing this physically can help us to communicate how we feel to God. Getting our body into the appropriate position when we pray can help us to be more open to God and to get through to him in a deeper way.

Praying to our Father

One of the things which come across very clearly in Jesus' long prayer here is the fact that he was praying to his Father. Jesus addressed God as his Father six times. We can learn a great deal from that, because once we grasp the fact that God is our loving heavenly Father, and not a distant God who is unrelated to us, then our prayer life becomes far more real and personal and alive. Jesus knew that God was his Father, who loved him, cared about him, provided for him and protected him: there was a warm, close relationship between Jesus and his Daddy. This is the sort of relationship which we too can have with God, through Jesus.

Now, there are a great many selfish, inadequate fathers around. Many Christians, having had such fathers, have never really experienced the kind of fatherhood which we are thinking about here. Their fathers never showed any *interest* in them, let alone showing them real love and care. Consequently it is difficult for these Christians to imagine or understand that God is their Daddy, simply because they have never really felt the warmth of a Daddy-type love. However, by the Holy Spirit God can heal them of that injury and gradually reveal to them how wonderful a Father God is. He is always interested in them, he is never too busy or too selfish to bother with them, and he always loves them and looks after them.

Those of us who are fathers ourselves know from our own experience how much it distresses us when we see our children suffer. How must God the Father have felt when he saw Jesus dying in terrible pain on the cross? The Father must have suffered anguish we can only begin to imagine – and both he and his Son went through that ordeal for our sakes.

So one aspect of the Father-Son relationship between God and Jesus is the warm, caring side of God's

36

character. But there is another aspect too. In his prayer, Jesus refers to God as his *holy Father* (John 17:11) and his *righteous Father* (verse 25). Jesus knew that his Daddy was also the holy, almighty God. This is something we need to grasp. God is not an over-indulgent parent who gives us everything we want without any discipline. Yes, he is our loving Father and longs to hear our prayers and delights in answering them, because he cares about us so much. But he is also our holy Father, and he will not tolerate sin in us. Our prayers will just bounce off the ceiling if we are not really committed to him, or if there is flagrant sin and selfishness in us which we refuse to acknowledge and confess.

There are three things, then, we should note about Jesus' prayer. First, it was *conversational* in that Jesus talked to God as his Father, quite naturally and without using any special language. There is still a tendency among Christians to talk to God in the language of the King James Version. This is unnecessary and inappropriate. It is worth noting that Jesus did not finish his prayer with the word 'Amen', which most Christians think is essential! But Jesus did not need a formal conclusion to his prayer, because it was a conversation, and one does not end a conversation with 'Amen'. There is no need for us to make our relationship with God so unnatural. This is particularly a problem for those of us who grew up in Christian homes.

The second thing to note about Jesus' prayer is that, although it was conversational, it was also respectful. He called God *holy Father* and *righteous Father*. Jesus did not have a casual, flippant attitude to God. Sadly, some Christians don't have enough respect for God. God does not answer flippant, casual prayers. We cannot treat God as someone who comes to help us when we need him, who just appears when we snap our fingers. Some Christians treat God as if he were some kind of cosmic butler, who hurries to do our bidding. He wants us to talk to him conversationally, but it is a conversation with someone for whom we have the very deepest respect. He is the Creator, and we are merely his creatures, and our prayers need to reflect this. The fact that prayer should be conversational and the fact that it should also be respectful are things which we must learn to hold in tension, because they are both important.

A third quality of Jesus' prayer to note is that it was *confident*. Jesus believed that his Father was listening to his prayer and he was sure that he would answer it. He was not afraid or worried. Sometimes we may feel that when we pray we are merely talking to ourselves, that nothing is getting through to God. But the truth is that he is always there, always listening to our prayers and eager to answer them.

Disaster or glory?

Jesus' prayer begins,

Father, the time has come. Glorify your Son, that your Son may glorify you.

(John 17:1)

This verse puzzles many people, because it appears that Jesus was asking something purely for himself. But he was not asking for glory or honour for his own sake, but for the benefit of the world. He was about to be crucified, and this was a form of execution reserved for runaway slaves, traitors and rebels. He was allowing himself to be associated with criminals; he was humbling himself utterly for the sake of our salvation. In effect he was saying to God, 'Glorify me, Father, and clearly demonstrate to the world that the shame and degradation I am going to suffer are in fact the way to eternal life; I pray that as I suffer this terrible death you will glorify me so that the world will see that you sent me and that they can have eternal life in me. Make out of this dreadful death something special and powerful and wonderful.' Jesus' ultimate humiliation, his death on the cross, was actually going to be his glorification.

To the disciples, Jesus' death on the cross seemed to be a disaster. Their Lord had been killed and they thought his mission on earth had failed. But in fact the cross was at the very centre of God's plan for the salvation of humankind. Had Jesus not died on the cross, no-one could have been saved from their sins, no-one could have been forgiven by God, no-one could have had eternal life, no-one could have received the Holy Spirit. Only through Jesus' death on the cross could God's plan work.

In our own lives, too, God can turn disasters into glory. We may be facing a difficult situation and things may seem to have gone wrong, but God may want to glorify himself through that situation. For example, someone may suffer a prolonged illness, and wonder why God has allowed it to happen. But it may be that while that person is at home in bed for weeks with nothing to do but be ill, God will speak to her in a new and dramatic way. The long-term result of that illness might be that God will be able to use her in his work much more effectively and powerfully than would have been the case had she not been forced to lie still and listen to him for weeks.

When the mother of James and John came to Jesus to ask that her sons might sit next to him when he came into his kingdom, Jesus replied, *You don't know what you are asking*. She was asking that her sons could share in Jesus' glory as his prime ministers. But his glory was to be death on a cross, so in effect she was asking that they might share the same death. Jesus asked the two disciples, *Can you drink the cup I am going to drink?* Not knowing what he was talking about, they answered, *We can*. (See Matthew 20:20–28.)

Jesus prayed,

Now this is eternal life: that they may know you, the only true God, and Jesus Christ, whom you have sent.

(John 17:3)

Eternal life is knowing God and Jesus. The Greek word translated 'know' means more than superficial knowledge, as in 'I know Joe Bloggs – he lives at the end of the street.' Knowing here means an *intimate relationship*, such as the love relationship between a married couple or between two very good friends. Jesus is not talking about knowing *about* God in a detached sort of way, but *knowing* him personally. Eternal life is everlasting life, but the most important aspect of the idea of eternal life is not its quantity (that is, length of time) but its quality, and the essence of that quality is that it is life spent in the immediate, personal presence of God.

Sometimes when I'm praying and experiencing God's presence with me and within me, I feel that I'm on to a huge secret which most people don't know about. I feel that I know the Lord, that he knows me, and that he's talking to me – not necessarily in actual words, but in feelings, thoughts and directions. Sometimes, after a prayer time like that, I almost feel like walking out into the street, going up to someone and saying, 'You'll never guess what! I've just spent some time being connected up to the universal power source! It lasted for several minutes, and it was wonderful! I'm not saying that I feel like that all the time, but when I do feel it, it's mind-boggling. Then eternal life seems so real to me and death seems like a mere transition from this life to another, to an even closer relationship with God.'

Eternal life is not a mere one-off thing, like a sheep being marked with dye to show who owns it: 'Yes, you're saved, you've got eternal life now, so off you go and get on with your life.' Rather, eternal life is about knowing God, and getting to know him better all the time, until finally we die physically and then know him better than ever. It is sad that many Christians are frightened by death and scared by life, because although they have given their lives over to God, their relationship with him on a day-by-day basis is fairly weak. This is not how it is meant to be; our Father does not want us to live and die in fear.

Like any other relationship, our knowing the Father has to be worked at and nourished if it is not to fade to the level of mere acquaintanceship. Marriage provides a clear analogy to this. It is quite often the case that the love between married couples fades with time if they take it for granted and don't keep putting coals on the fire of their relationship. They are still living in the same house and are still legally married to each other, but they are no longer sharing their lives as deeply as they used to. Often this happens because the couple become so overwhelmed by the demands of raising their children that they no longer have time to nourish their marriage, and as a result, when the children finally leave home the parents find that they no longer really know each other. Something similar can happen in the Christian life. We can become so busy doing our work for God that we no longer have time to know him. The deep, close relationship which we once had with him begins to fade and grow cold. But Jesus, busy though he was with his ministry, knew the importance of setting time aside to devote to his relationship with God. He knew what eternal life was and he knew it was not something which happens only after death. Rather, it is something which the Father wants us to possess now – that is, the personal experience of God.

Two kinds of trouble

At the top of Jesus' list of prayer items were his followers, that is, his first disciples and all people who would believe in him down the ages:

Holy Father, protect them by the power of your name – the name you gave me – so that they may be one as we are one … My prayer is not that you take them out of the world but that you protect them from the evil one. They are not of the world, even as I am not of it.

(John 17:11, 15–16)

There are some Christians who have somehow gained the impression that God has promised to make their lives absolutely free of problems, difficulties and suffering. As we saw in chapter 2, Jesus never promised us that. In fact, he told us that being a Christian would not be easy: *In this world you will have trouble.* But he also told us, *Take heart! I have overcome the world* (John 16:33). God does not take us out of the world, but Jesus has won victory over the world for us, and God will protect us from the evil one.

Christians suffer in two ways. The first is the suffering they experience simply by being human in a fallen, sinful world. We suffer the consequences of sin, just as non-Christians do. Christians are not immune to the common cold, for example. When economic recessions occur because of people's greediness and selfishness, some Christians will lose their jobs. Irresponsible, sinful humankind is polluting the global environment, and Christians have to endure the contaminated air and water just like anyone else. God has never promised to take us out of the real world and surround us with soft cushions.

Secondly, Christians suffer by being Christians. This world is dominated by the devil, and when we become Christians we are deliberately rejecting him and his value system and embracing Jesus Christ and his righteousness. The world is like a great river, and it generally flows in the direction the devil wants it to flow in. When we become Christians we turn around and swim against the flow of the world, and so inevitably life becomes a constant battle. The devil doesn't like being rejected, and so he does his level best to destroy our faith. He cannot rob us of our salvation in Jesus, but he can rob us of the joy of it. He wants to stop us enjoying being Christians, he wants to make the Christian life dull and miserable, so that eventually we give up trying to be true disciples of Jesus.

The devil tries to stop us praying and reading the Bible by distracting us or making it difficult. Among Christian fellowships, the devil will take personality clashes and use them to distort and damage the life of the church. He will even try to stop us going to church at all. Have you ever felt reluctant to go to church on a Sunday? You think it's going to be boring, or there is someone in the fellowship you find so irritating that you're afraid you'll say something awful to him, or there is something in the service which you feel is too challenging for you. But have you noticed that once you are at church, in the presence of God and his worshipping people, you are very glad you are there? All those feelings of reluctance were from the devil, who wanted you to miss out on the blessing you get at church. Or else, have you noticed that visitors always seem to want to come to see you on Sundays, so that you won't be able to get to church? Invitations to see people always seem to be on Sundays, don't they?

All this rubbish from the devil is bound to be part of our experience as Christians, because he is determined to do all he can to oppose us. Paul described this vividly when he wrote,

We are hard pressed on every side, but not crushed; perplexed, but not in despair; persecuted, but not abandoned; struck down, but not destroyed.

(2 Corinthians 4:8–9)

Jesus has told us that in this world we will experience trouble and pressure. We should not be surprised about it, and we should learn to recognize when the devil is at work and claim the victory over him in the name of Jesus. Jesus did not promise to keep us free from attack by the enemy, but he did promise to give us victory over those attacks.

A prayer for unity

Jesus prayed about the disciples,

I have given them the glory that you gave me, that they may be one as we are one: I in them and you in me. May they be brought to complete unity to let the world know that you sent me and have loved them even as you loved me.

(John 17:22–23)

Jesus wanted his disciples to be united. He knew what a selfish, bickering bunch they were, frequently arguing about who was top dog. But this is also a prayer for Jesus' disciples in all ages, that they will be united in him. I don't believe that Jesus wanted us all to be the same; it is quite possible to have diversity within unity. Rather, Jesus wanted the church to be united in purpose and in commitment to him. Sometimes this passage is used as a basis for the modern ecumenical movement and to argue that all churches should be united in one organizational structure. But I don't think Jesus' prayer necessarily implies that; I believe Jesus was talking about his people being one in himself, one in purpose and activity and power. Whether or not there should be different denominations is a secondary issue.

When the church is truly united, it is awesomely powerful. The devil is rightly afraid of that power, and so he goes to great lengths to disrupt Christian unity. He tempts Christians to gossip about one another and so spread lies and half-truths. He tempts them to criticize one another, with the result that their eyes are fixed solely on the negative things about one another and not the positive things.

One of the biggest lies which the devil has foisted on the British church in recent years is the mistaken idea that God will send the power of his Spirit on churches only when all their members have got absolutely right with God. There are many Christians today who believe this, and yet when one considers it, it is an absurd notion. How many of us can ever say that we are sure that we have got all the sin and hurt and bondage in our lives thoroughly sorted out by God? If anyone does dare to say that they have, it only goes to show that they are naïve, and they don't understand the subtleties of human sin and how high God's standards of spiritual purity are. None of us is ever completely sorted out, so how can it be the case that a church fellowship can ever be completely sorted out? If God sent his power only when everything was perfect, all churches everywhere would be completely powerless. If we think we have to wait until everything is put right before we can see God's power, we will never have the faith to see things happening, which is precisely the state which the enemy wants us to be in.

The result of this attitude, on the one hand, a lack of spiritual power, because our expectations are low, and on the other hand a critical spirit. People become frustrated that nothing is happening in their church, and so it must be because *A* hasn't got his life sorted out, and *B* needs to get her priorities right, and *C* needs to repent of his besetting sins. 'If only the worship in the services was right, if only we had better preachers, if only the housegroups were more ably led, if only the church leaders were in touch with God, if only certain people left the church, then everything would be all right and God would move among us in power.'

The truth is very different. Jesus does not wait for us all to become perfect in every way before he will act. He takes us where we are, not where we should be, and he does something with us now, today, not at some unspecified, long-awaited day in the future. Of course, Jesus wants us all to be seeking ever greater spiritual purity. He wants us to be continually seeking to please him more and more with the way we are living. He wants the prayer of all of us to be, 'Lord, I want to be right with you, I want to be holy, I want to be pure.' But in the meantime, despite our many imperfections, he still uses us for his glory. He does not ask us to be totally right with him before he will use us; he asks us to be *ready* to be used, which is a very different thing. He merely asks us to be open to him, and to want him to work in our lives and in our churches.

Sometimes the devil will try to divide fellowships in ways which are obviously bad, such as criticism and complaining. People say things like: 'I wish they wouldn't do A.' 'I wish they would do B.' 'Why is C allowed to happen?' 'Why isn't D happening?' 'The services are too long.' 'The services are too short.' 'The worship is too lively.' 'The worship isn't lively enough.'

But at other times the devil divides churches by using things which, in themselves, are good. For example, one group of people in a church may think that Project A would be a great thing for the church to do, while another thinks Project B would be great. The fellowship has limited financial and human resources, and so it cannot do both A and B simultaneously. The leaders have to make a choice between the two, and they go for Project A. The advocates of A are delighted, but the B enthusiasts are annoyed and disappointed. They start murmuring, 'The leaders obviously aren't close enough to God. We know that God wanted the church to do Project B, but they went for A. They can't hear God's voice properly. Maybe it's time we had different

46

leaders.' Both *A* and *B* were good and worthwhile projects, but the church could undertake only one of them. Because the *B* backers will not accept the leaders' decision with good grace, the devil has the opportunity to turn a good idea into a cause of division.

Unity in the church is vital for it to do its God-given job properly, and we all have our part to play in making that unity. We particularly need to watch what we say about other people. Even when we criticize them in a light-hearted, semi-joking way, we are doing damage to the body of the fellowship, because our remarks may plant seeds of doubt and confusion and criticism in the hearts of those who hear them. Many of us need to confess that we have been agents of disunity through our attitudes and words, and we need to ask God for forgiveness and the ability to build up the body rather than to break it down.

When we get to heaven we will stand in front of Jesus and he will say to some of us, 'Why did you spend two years of your life worrying yourself silly because you felt that they were singing the songs at the wrong speed in your church? I had important work for you to do during that time, and instead you wasted your energy on such a trivial matter.'

When that time comes we will feel very foolish, hang our heads and say, 'Sorry, Lord.' But right now, these trivial matters seem so big to us that they can dominate our lives. That is precisely where the devil wants us to be: wasting our energy over minuscule, divisive issues, while the really important issues in our lives and churches are ignored. We need to recognize the game the devil is playing and refuse to take part. We need to rebuke and reject him and ask God to make us agents of unity and purpose in the church.

Holiness first

Jesus prayed,

Sanctify them by the truth; your word is truth.

(John 17:17)

The Greek word *hagiazō*, translated 'sanctify' here, literally means 'to make holy'. Jesus was asking God to make his followers *holy*. We should note that he did not ask God to make us *happy*. Much of the time we assume that it is God's basic intention to organize things so that we are happy, so that we have no problems or difficulties to face. We pray, 'Lord, please take this away and take that away and make me feel a bit better; please sort things out so that I feel okay.' Christians think this way because they have been brainwashed by the modern culture around them, which believes that personal fulfilment and happiness are the highest good and the goal of human life. But Jesus prayed that we would be made holy and pure by God. It is often the case that the very 'problems' which we want God to take away from us are the things he is using to make us more holy people. God's priority is to make us holy. By becoming more holy we will also become happier people, because we will be closer to God. But happiness is the consequence of holiness. In God's scheme of things holiness comes first.

Jesus had already prayed for his immediate band of disciples, but then he went on:

My prayer is not for them alone. I pray also for those who will believe in me through their message.

(John 17:20)

Jesus was here praying for all Christians throughout the centuries, because we all believe in Jesus as a result of the message which the apostles preached back in the first century AD. The church in Britain today is directly descended from the church which the apostles founded in Jerusalem. In other words, Jesus was praying for you and me, for every Christian. He was and is bothered about us personally. That prayer was prayed by Jesus almost two thousand years ago, but God is still answering it in my life and yours. It is exciting and reassuring to know that our lives have been and are being touched by a prayer from Jesus' own lips.

Chapter 4

Faith under pressure

When he had finished praying, Jesus left with his disciples and crossed the Kidron Valley. On the other side there was an olive grove, and he and his disciples went into it.

Now Judas, who betrayed him, knew the place, because Jesus had often met there with his disciples. So Judas came to the grove, guiding a detachment of soldiers and some officials from the chief priests and Pharisees. They were carrying torches, lanterns and weapons.

(John 18:1)

Jerusalem was built on a hill, and facing it across the Kidron Valley was the Mount of Olives. Jesus and the disciples now went into the valley and into the garden of Gethsemane on the Mount. Jesus left the city just as the people would have been slaughtering their Passover lambs. An ancient document which was written about thirty years after Jesus' death says that at that time almost 300,000 lambs were sacrificed at the Passover in Jerusalem. Some of the blood of each of those lambs would have been poured on the altar in the temple, and behind the altar there was a well into which the blood would run, and from there it would run through a channel out of the city and into the Kidron Valley. Since so many lambs were slaughtered, often the river actually turned blood-red. It is quite possible that as Jesus walked across the valley the water would have been bloody, and this would have served as a potent symbol of the brutal and bloody death which Jesus, the ultimate Passover lamb, was very soon about to suffer.

Verse 2 tells us that Jesus and the disciples often went to Gethsemane. It would have been their haven of peace and quiet where they could pray and where Jesus would teach them. It was probably owned by a wealthy Jerusalem man who had given Jesus the free use of it as a retreat. And here Jesus waited for Judas and the soldiers to come for him and take him back to the city and all the suffering he would soon have to endure there.

While he waited in the garden for Judas to come, Jesus experienced what must have been the most acute pressure of his entire life. He knew that for the sake of humankind he had to go through the agony of death on a cross, and yet, though he was the Son of God, he was also a human being, and he experienced the natural dread of facing a painful death that any person would feel. Gethsemane became the crucible in which his faith in God was tested as never before in his life. During this agonizing time of waiting, his whole relationship with God was put to the test. Would he obey God, or would he take the easy way out and avoid death? His reason for being born into the world was to suffer this sacrificial death for our salvation, and yet that knowledge would not have made the imminent reality of that death any easier to contemplate.

We have a tendency to think that because Jesus was God, his suffering wasn't quite as real as ours is. But he was completely human as well as being completely divine. There is no doubt that his agony of spirit at Gethsemane was acute and intense. What Jesus had to endure makes the suffering in the lives of most Christians look insignificant. We may have problems and difficulties, but they are nothing compared to what Jesus faced that night on the Mount of Olives. We need to get

51

our own suffering in perspective, or we will become filled with self-pity and despair, when in actual fact we have a great deal to be thankful for.

The amazing way in which Jesus rose to the challenge he confronted shows a level of spiritual maturity which we will never attain, but it is at least a goal towards which we can aim, an example for all men and women who want to walk with God. There are dimensions of spiritually, realized most conspicuously in the life of Jesus, which are far beyond the experience of the great majority of Christians, and yet God wants to draw us towards those dimensions. I am not talking about signs and wonders, although we can be excited about them if God gives them to us. I am talking about a spiritual maturity, an inner resolve and tranquillity, a relationship with Jesus Christ which brings power into our innermost being and enables us to live as sons and daughters of God our King. As I consider my own life and the lives of most of the Christians I know, I recognize that we are a million miles from that kind of spiritual dimension. Many Christians think they have somehow arrived spiritually, but in fact they have only begun to experience the wonderful things that God wants to give us in our innermost personality.

Peace through submission

Jesus' attitude is expressed most clearly in John 18:11. When Simon Peter cut off the high priest's servant's right ear with a sword,

Jesus commanded Peter, 'Put your sword away! Shall I not drink the cup the Father has given me?'

(John 18:11)

Jesus was absolutely sure of what his destiny was, of what God wanted him to do: he knew that his cup was a cup of suffering. He had known for many years that he had been born into the world in order to die a sacrificial death, and he had often told his disciples about this. He refers to it a number of times in John's Gospel. His will was totally submitted to the Father's will.

If we are honest with ourselves, we will admit that when we face pressure and stress, whether it be at work, or at home, or in our spiritual lives, or in our emotional or physical health, what often happens is that we simply cave in. Along comes the pressure, and we just fall apart under its weight. We remain in this shattered state for a few weeks or months, and finally the problematic circumstances which caused the cave-in change and the pressure is taken away, and so we feel more or less all right again. We may kid ourselves that we coped with the pressure through our faith in God, but in fact we recovered from the problem only because it went away, not because we faced up to it and coped with it head-on.

But Jesus genuinely knew how to cope with pressure; his faith in God was of the calibre which could stand the stress. How did he do it? His secret was that he was sure that he was doing the Father's will. His attitude was, 'I have given the control of my life over to my Father. I don't make the decisions; he does. I'm not the captain of my soul; he is. My chief desire is to please the Father, and so I will be absolutely obedient to his will.'

There is great security and peace in the knowledge that we are doing the right thing, even when that thing means that we have to face pressure and pain or even death, as was the case with Jesus. We may have a difficult and dark valley to walk through, but if we know that that is what the Lord wants us to do, then, whatever the problems and pressures which beset us, we can know a God-given tranquillity and sense of purpose. Admittedly, it takes most Christians quite some time to arrive at this state, because it entails a certain amount of spiritual maturity. But when we reach it we can have a confidence which nothing else can give us. We have peace in the midst of life's pressures because we know that we are in God's hands and we are walking with him. And having reached this point in our spiritual development, we often have to keep coming back to it, because there is a tendency for us to slip away from it.

We discover a remarkable liberty when our attitude is, 'Lord, I won't do what I want to do; I'll do what you want me to do.' For example, if someone has hurt us in some way and we feel angry and injured, our natural, sinful reaction is to want to retaliate. But if we surrender the matter to God and ask, 'Lord, how do you feel about this?' we will be able to forgive and love the person, because the Lord will make us feel as he feels about it. Jesus found that there is an ultimate freedom in complete slavery to God; that is one of the paradoxes which are crucial to the Christian life. If we completely submit to God's will, we will experience a greater freedom than we could ever have otherwise.

Of course, our natural, sinful natures rebel against that submission; we want to be our own bosses. In every Christian there is a naughty little child who throws temper tantrums whenever the Father says, 'No, don't do that; I want you to do this instead.' We think we know best and we like to have things our own way. But the truth is that this is self-defeating, because by resisting God, by withholding our complete submission to his will, we are creating tension in our lives. Until we submit to him completely, there will always be a battle going on inside us between what God is telling us to do and what our selfish desires tell us to do. God does not force us to submit; it is a choice we must make ourselves. God wants us to submit because that is what is best for us. We can never know the peace which Jesus had in the face of pressure if we do not first humbly accept God's lordship over us.

In control under pressure

John 18:3 reads,

So Judas came to the grove, guiding a detachment of soldiers and some officials from the chief priests and Pharisees. They were carrying torches, lanterns and weapons.

The Greek word translated 'detachment' means a military unit of either 1,000 men or 200. They sent a force of at least 200 temple guards, plus a group of officials and priests, to arrest Jesus, one unarmed Galilean rabbi! So great had Jesus' reputation become that his enemies felt they needed an overwhelming show of force in order to arrest him. Perhaps, too, they were afraid that Jesus might have a large group of followers with him who would resist his arrest.

Jesus could easily have avoided being arrested. The soldiers with their lanterns and torches must have been very visible and audible as they approached, and Jesus could have slipped away into the olive grove and evaded them. But instead he came out of the shadows and asked them, *Who is it you want?*

They replied that they were looking for Jesus of Nazareth, and Jesus answered, *I am he* (verses 4–5).

When he said this, the people who had come to arrest him *drew back and fell to the ground.* Some Christians believe that this was a manifestation of Jesus' divine power – that in saying *I am he* he was using the Old Testament name of God, I AM, thereby identifying himself as God – and the effect of this was to knock the people over by the mere power of his name. But personally I don't agree with that interpretation. I don't think there was anything supernatural about this incident. It was simply that the soldiers and officials and priests were afraid of Jesus and were so startled by his sudden appearance from the shadows that their front rank stepped back from him in surprise, and those behind them were pushed over by this in a sort of domino effect.

It took a very special kind of confidence for Jesus to step forward and say, 'I am the one you are looking for.' These people were there to take him away to have him killed; he had no illusions about that. And yet he knew that the time had come for him to lay down his life, and he surrendered himself without flinching. He had the supreme confidence which comes from knowing what God wants, and doing it obediently. This was not brash arrogance but a calm, inner strength.

One thing that comes across clearly in this passage is that Jesus was the one who was really in control. By the world's thinking it should have been the mob who were in control, since there were a lot more of them. But it was Jesus who dominated the situation. He had decided where they were to find him; he had deliberately gone to Gethsemane, where he often went, knowing that Judas knew he would be there. And really they did not arrest him, but rather he gave himself up to them. The initiative was his. He even told the soldiers to let the disciples go free, and they did as he said.

That sort of inner peace and control is what God wants to give all of us when our faith is under pressure. The first thing we tend to lose control of in crisis situations is our tongue. When we are anxious we start to say things we don't really mean. I have had some weird conversations with frightened people in my dentist's waiting room and during aeroplane journeys. In those situations people get nervous and say some strange things. And yet, because Jesus is totally sure of the Father's will and knows that he is obeying it, he has complete control of himself, including his tongue. He says what needs to be said, neither more nor less.

Consistent under pressure

The fact that Jesus' disciples escaped arrest by his

request was the fulfilment of a word he had spoken perhaps as much as two years previously: *I shall lose none of all that [God] has given me* (John 6:39). Jesus was perfectly consistent even in the face of death itself. What he had promised to do he would do. He was soon going to die, but he still cared about his disciples, as he always had done.

Many of us have to confess that we fail to be consistent under pressure. Often, when pressure and problems come, we fall apart at the seams and all our promises and good intentions count for nothing. We may have committed ourselves to doing a particular job in our church, but when the going gets a little tough we think we have the perfect right to break our promises and drop everything, leaving other people stranded and overburdened. Some people seem to think that God expects them to be joyful, mature, approachable Christians only when things are going well; when things are difficult they are allowed to behave in ways which one does not expect of Christians. They seem to think that having a bad day gives them the right to lose their temper with people and to be selfish and disagreeable.

Now, of course, there are times when Christians are on the receiving end of such acute pressure that they really cannot cope with their commitments and it is right for them to drop a few things. It is usually fairly clear to all concerned when that really is the case: for example, someone's marriage may be in serious trouble, or they may be suffering from clinical depression, or they may have some other grave health problem. However, it is quite often the case that Christians break their promises for no very good reason, simply because things have got a little difficult for them. Rather than dropping their commitments, they should trust God, weather the storm and carry on with their work for the Lord. We need to be people whose word is reliable. If we say we will do something, people should be able to feel enough confidence in us to trust us to do it.

Jesus is our model of perfect consistency. He didn't use pressure as an excuse to lower his spiritual and moral standards. Whatever his circumstances were, he always kept his promises and always behaved in a consistent, righteous, God-pleasing manner.

Concerned under pressure

Another striking thing about Jesus in this incident is his concern for other people. He was concerned about the disciples, and asked that they might be allowed to go free. Then, after Simon Peter had hacked off the right ear of the high priest's servant, Jesus told him to put his sword away and, as we read in Luke 22:51, he then healed the wounded man's ear.

There is something comic about Peter's brand of heroism. He suffered from a kind of foot and mouth disease – he was for ever opening his mouth and putting his foot in it, rushing in where angels fear to tread. There were the disciples with their two puny little swords, facing 200 soldiers. What did he do? Did he cower with fear and think about surrendering? No, he decided that since they had apparently come to kill Jesus and the disciples, he might as well take as many of the enemy with him as he could. So he rushed into the crowd of soldiers, officials and priests, hacking wildly with his sword, trying to do as much damage to as many people as possible! Malchus, the servant of the high priest, didn't duck away quickly enough, and so he lost his ear. He was lucky; it could have been his neck!

Jesus intervened and called Peter off, and, amazingly, healed Malchus's ear. Jesus was in control. He had no intention of letting Peter turn this incident into a squalid bloodbath. And more than that, even though Malchus was one of his enemies who intended to have him put to death, he was still concerned for the injured man. Most of us, facing the prospect of imminent death, might have refrained from Peter's foolish violence (possibly just through fear), but how many of us could have shown such concern for one of our enemies? Jesus was so secure in his relationship with God and in the knowledge that he was doing God's will that he still had the ability to care for others, even in the midst of such a personally threatening situation. Under such immense pressure Jesus was still capable of reaching out to others, and of caring about their needs rather than his own safety.

The confidence, control and concern which Jesus showed at this time are an example to us all, and it makes us acutely aware of how great a gulf there is between him and ourselves. But this example should not depress us and make us feel worthless. It is a goal towards which we ourselves can aspire, since we have the Spirit of Jesus living within us. Jesus Christ is in us. By opening up to him, so that he has a greater and greater lordship over our lives, we can hope that we will, by his Spirit, be increasingly able to emulate Jesus' behaviour under pressure.

Chapter 5

Annas and Caiaphas

Then the detachment of soldiers with its commander and the Jewish officials arrested Jesus. They bound him and brought him first to Annas, who was the father-in-law of Caiaphas, the high priest that year. Caiaphas was the one who had advised the Jews that it would be good if one man died for the people.

(John 18:12–14)

The rest of John 18 reminds me a little of a TV soap, where the action moves rapidly from one location to another and back again. In verses 12–14 we see Jesus being questioned by Annas; in verses 15–18 the scene switches to Peter and his first denial of Jesus; then in verses 19–24 we are with Jesus again, and he has been brought before Caiaphas, the high priest. Next we go back to Peter in verses 25–27, when he denies Jesus twice more; finally in verses 28–40 we are with Jesus again as he is questioned by Pontius Pilate. There is a 'Meanwhile, back at the ranch …' quality to this second part of the chapter. Verse 19 begins, *Meanwhile, the high priest questioned Jesus …*

First of all Jesus was bound and brought before Annas, the father-in-law of the high priest. Annas was a very rich and powerful man. His family had, through bribery, dominated the religious establishment for generations and had produced many high priests. Annas was an extremely unsavoury character. As a matter of fact, he was so hated by the Jewish people of the time that his name was used as slang for donkey dung! Annas was a cynical political manipulator who cared about nothing except maintaining the power and wealth of his own family. He wanted his family to control the high priesthood because the high priests had authority.

Next Jesus was taken to Caiaphas, the high priest, who questioned him *about his disciples and his teaching* (John 18:19). This was all completely out of order, since it was illegal for the Jews to hold any kind of trial at night. In answer to the high priest Jesus said,

I have spoken openly to the world … I always taught in synagogues or at the temple, where all the Jews come together. I said nothing in secret. Why question me? Ask those who heard me. Surely they know what I said.

(verses 20–21)

Jesus had always done everything in an open manner; they had no right to question him in this secretive way at night. Their response to this was to hit him in the face.

'If I said something wrong,' Jesus replied, 'testify as to what is wrong. But if I spoke the truth, why did you strike me?'

(verse 23)

The whole procedure was illegal not only because it was being held at night but also because it was flouting the rules of Jewish trials. One of the basic requirements of Jewish law was that all the evidence had to be reviewed and all the witnesses had to be questioned before the accused himself was interrogated, so Caiaphas was completely out of order to question Jesus.

Closed minds

One thing which is patently obvious from this chapter of John's Gospel is that Jesus was being interrogated by people whose minds were completely closed. They had already decided that they wanted to get rid of him. Nothing he could have said would have made any difference at that point, so that was why he refused to answer their questions. The prophet Isaiah had referred to this when he wrote,

He was led like a lamb to the slaughter, and as a sheep before her shearers is silent, so he did not open his mouth.

(Isaiah 53:7)

Closed minds among non-Christians can be a great barrier to successful evangelism, but Christians too can be guilty of the same sin. Some Christians have pet doctrines and opinions which no amount of contrary evidence or argument can change. Their attitude is, 'I have made up my mind on this issue, so don't confuse me with the facts.' They think that if they don't know anything about it and they haven't experienced it, then it must be wrong. One can imagine the sense of frustration which Jesus must have felt in the presence of people whose minds were so closed.

Corrupt motivation

The motivation behind the high priest's questions was corrupt and base; he didn't want to know the truth about Jesus. The high priest asked him about *his disciples and his teaching* (John 18:19). He wanted to know how many disciples Jesus had and whether his teaching was politically dangerous. How great a threat to their authority was he? All the rulers cared about was their own power and security. They lived a comfortable existence, so long as they pleased the Romans; they weren't going to allow Jesus to upset the apple-cart. His popularity with the people was seen as a threat to their own position.

Corrupt motivation is something which we Christians today should watch out for. Sometimes we need to stop and ask ourselves why we want something. We say we think it will be good for the church, but if we look inside ourselves honestly, we will see corrupt, selfish motives.

For example, when we see something new going on in the church nationally or within our own church fellowship, and we find it suspect, we should not be hasty to condemn it. We should ask ourselves honestly why we find it disturbing. Can we really be sure that it is unbiblical or ungodly? Or is it simply that it is something new to us, something we have never experienced before? Is the problem simply that we don't like new, disturbing things – even when it's God who is doing them?

Or worse still, do we resent what is happening because we secretly perceive it as a threat to us and our ministry within the church? Are we afraid that some of the prestige which we presently enjoy will be drawn to the people doing the new things instead? If we are church leaders, are we afraid that some of the sheep of our flock will be enticed away from us to other pastures?

To take another example, we may be keen on high-tech gadgets, and we may nag the leadership of our church to buy this or that new computer software package or satellite link-up which has come on the market recently. We argue that it will be very useful to the church. But perhaps we need to ask ourselves whether the enormous cost of the gadget is really justified by the actual benefits which it will bring. Wouldn't the money have been better spent, for example, in helping members of the church who are in financial difficulty? How will a church member who is desperately struggling (and perhaps failing) to make ends meet feel when we stand up in church one Sunday morning to tell the fellowship that the church has just bought a wonderful new gizmo costing hundreds or thousands of pounds, when the equipment which it has replaced was really quite adequate?

Or perhaps there is a need for someone to fill a particular leadership role in our church, and we have been dropping subtle hints that if asked to fill it, we would be willing. Why do we want to take on that leadership role? Is it really because we want to serve God and the church, or is it because we think it will satisfy some emotional need which we have? Perhaps we secretly feel inadequate and we want a leadership position to increase our sense of worth. Or perhaps we simply think we are an important person in the church whose status ought to be officially recognized.

We need to be honest with God and with ourselves. What is our real motivation? When God shows us that it is not as pure as it might be, we must say sorry to him and ask him to give us godly, wholesome, unselfish motivation instead.

Criminal manipulation

The high priest manipulated the situation in a way which was thoroughly criminal. He set Jesus' legal rights aside. The trial was conducted at night, no witnesses were called, and Jesus was not allowed to speak in his own defence. Finally, when Jesus protested, he was struck in the face, supposedly for failing to be courteous to the high priest. Caiaphas thought nothing of flouting the law for his own purposes, but he was outraged by what he saw as a breach of etiquette by Jesus – though, of course, what Jesus had said was eminently true and fair. Caiaphas probably wanted Jesus to be much more deferential to him. In short, Caiaphas and his cronies were out to manipulate the situation to get the result they wanted. They cared nothing for truth or legality; all they wanted was their own way.

All of us are tempted to be manipulative at times, to try to arrange events and the lives of others to get the result which we want. Sometimes the goal of our manipulation is ostensibly a good one, and in these cases the end seems to justify the means. This sin features more prominently in the behaviour of some people than in that of others. For some people, manipulating circumstances and other people is a way of life.

Even some Christians can be manipulative. They work tirelessly to get people to agree with their point of view, to get people to do what they want them to do. They never stop to ask themselves, 'Does God actually want what I am agitating for? Will it actually benefit the people concerned? And even if the end is right, does that justify the means I am employing?'

It is never right to manipulate people. Manipulation means a blatant disregard for people as individuals made in the image of God. If we want to influence people, all we can do is tell them what we believe to be the truth, and prayerfully leave it up to them to think it through and make their own decision.

In defence of Peter

I feel that biblical commentators and preachers are often too hard on Peter. They ask, 'How could Peter deny Jesus three times, after he had spent three years with him, living with him, talking with him, getting to know him as a friend, seeing him do amazing miracles, and coming to recognize that he was the Messiah? He had been so privileged, and yet all it took was a question from the girl on duty at the door to the high priest's courtyard completely to unravel Peter's commitment to Jesus.'

However, I think the question we need to ask is, how would we have responded if we had been in Peter's shoes? He was a fallible human being, and as such his best intentions had a tendency not always to work out in his weakest moments. He had just seen a big gang of soldiers arrest his beloved Lord, and he was terrified that he too would be seized and butchered.

And the temptation to deny Jesus was made all the more powerful by the way the girl phrased her question. She did not say, 'Are you a disciple of Jesus?' Faced with a straight question like that, Peter may well have bluntly answered that he was a disciple. But what she actually said was, *You are not one of his disciples, are you?* (John 18:25). In other words, 'Surely a big, strong, normal-looking chap like you couldn't possibly be one of Jesus' followers?' The subtlety of the question put Peter in an invidious position, and he squirmed inside, and finally came out with a negative reply. The fact that the girl had posed her question almost as a statement that he was not a disciple made it all the easier for Peter simply to agree with her. This was Peter's first betrayal of Jesus, and that little step of betrayal led the way to the two later betrayals which were crystal-clear and positive. The betrayal developed from 'Well, maybe I'm not one of his followers' to 'I'm definitely not one of his followers.'

We should hesitate to condemn Peter for this, because we often demonstrate a similar pattern. The devil still works against our faith today as he worked against Peter's. If someone were to ask us directly, 'Are you a Christian?' we would not find it difficult to answer 'Yes'. Indeed, any other answer would be a lie. But such questions are not usually couched in such easy, direct terms. If someone says something like, 'Surely you're not one of these over-emotional, Bible-thumping, fundamentalist Christians, are you?' it is less clear how we ought to reply. What the person is really talking about is someone who genuinely loves Jesus and takes the Bible seriously as the Word of God, but the emotive words he has used are ones we would rather he did not apply to us. So we answer that no, we are not quite that sort of Christian, knowing that he may thereby gain the impression that we do not get excited about God and we don't believe the Bible. By being put in an awkward position by the nature of the question, we have replied in a way which has partially undermined our Christian witness, and as a result of that minor betrayal we may be trapped into further betrayals, until it is difficult for us to maintain any kind of Christian witness with that person at all. It would be better, at this point, to take the initiative and explain briefly what we do believe, rather than allowing our accuser to set the agenda.

Peter was just plain scared of being crucified for his faith in Jesus, and who wouldn't have been? Most of us don't expect to have to pay such a high price for being Christians, so we should not rush to condemn Peter and other Christians throughout the ages who have been in similar positions. We too are scared about being identified as Christians, and that fear takes two forms: fear of exclusion and fear of ridicule. These two fears can tempt us to betray Jesus.

Usually that betrayal is subtle and increases gradually over a long period of time. We may have given our lives to Jesus many years ago, and he has changed us and helped us in all sorts of ways. Yet we may now be faced with a situation in which people are constantly hostile to God, and we find it very difficult to be bold and clear about our Christian commitment. By failing to identify ourselves positively as Christians we are betraying Jesus. I believe that this is particularly a problem for men, because the whole drift of male culture and psychology is against admitting to our emotional and spiritual side, or to any form of weakness. Men are under pressure from their peers to appear worldly and 'cool' and dominant, all attitudes which cut across the grain of a genuine commitment to Jesus.

It is so easy to fall into the subtle trap of betrayal by a mere glance or word or action. By a small act we may distance ourselves from Christians, because the cost of identifying ourselves with them among our workmates or neighbours is too great. It is always easier to go along with the flow than to swim against the tide. In most walks of life there is a pressure to conform to the world's pattern and to dissociate ourselves from Jesus and commitment to him.

Peter faced the ultimate pressure to conform: the threat of death. He was under intense stress; all it took was an unexpected question from a girl, and his witness collapsed. Many of us would have collapsed in precisely the same way, so we should sympathize with him rather than condemn him. Poor Peter. He really did love Jesus and didn't want to betray him, but his fear got the better of him. No wonder he went out of the courtyard and wept bitter tears of shame (see Luke 22:62).

Betrayal is like an insidious disease which grows within us without our noticing it. We may have betrayed the Lord in small ways, and those small betrayals can grow into large ones, resulting in coldness and half-heartedness towards Jesus, and finally the ultimate betrayal of turning away from him and giving up being a Christian. We have to keep a sharp lookout for inner betrayal.

Chapter 6

Jesus the King on trial

Then the Jews led Jesus from Caiaphas to the palace of the Roman governor. By now it was early morning, and to avoid ceremonial uncleanness the Jews did not enter the palace; they wanted to be able to eat the Passover. So Pilate came out to them and asked, 'What charges are you bringing against this man?'

'If he were not a criminal,' they replied, 'we would not have handed him over to you.'

Pilate said, 'Take him yourselves and judge him by your own law.'

'But we have no right to execute anyone,' the Jews objected. This happened so that the words Jesus had spoken indicating the kind of death he was going to die would be fulfilled.

(John 18:28–32)

Pilate's palace would have been full of things which were ceremonially unclean to the Jews (paintings, statues, 'unclean' foods and so on), so they were unwilling to go into it, because in doing so they would have made themselves unclean. It is interesting that even so early in the morning, Pilate was willing to go out of his house to speak to the Jews. If it had been an ordinary group of locals he would doubtless have told them to come back and see him later in the day. But these particular Jews were powerful figures in Jerusalem, and he had no wish to alienate them, so he went out to see them.

Who's in control?

It is important to remember that even at this point, Jesus was the one who was truly in control of the situation. Verse 32 says,

This happened so that the words Jesus had spoken indicating the kind of death he was going to die would be fulfilled.

Jesus had told the disciples that he was going to be crucified, and this interview with Pilate was part of the journey to that cross. Jesus knew what was going to happen, he knew it had to happen, and he was permitting it to happen. To observers at the time it would have appeared that anyone but Jesus was in control. They would have said that Pilate, representing the Roman Empire, was in control, or that the Jewish religious leaders were really controlling the situation; Jesus would have been seen as merely the victim of a conspiracy. However, through the suffering of his Son, God was working his purposes out. From a merely human perspective Jesus was in a desperate plight: he was surrounded by enemies who were determined to do away with him, and Pilate, the legal authority, was prepared to let him die in order to please the Jewish leadership. Jesus knew he was on his way to die an excruciating death on a cross. There was absolutely no doubt about it. And yet he was not flustered or panicky, he was not reduced to a cowering, snivelling wreck; he simply endured it all in silence and dignity, knowing that he was doing God's will.

If we really want it, we too can have the peace which Jesus had in the pressurized, stressful, frustrating, frightening situations in our own lives. We may face pressure at work, or experience the shock of unemployment, or have problems in our families. A loved one may be seriously ill or even die. But in the midst of all that pressure, the Jesus who lives in us is the Jesus who is in control. We need to realize that when our world seems to be falling apart at the seams, Jesus is still in us. He is still in charge, and he is still Lord.

It is likely that Pilate himself had heard about Jesus, about the huge following he had among the people, about his reputation as a Teacher, and about the miracles he had done. The whole of Palestine had heard about Jesus. So when Pilate asked, *What charges are you bringing against this man?* (John 18:29), he may have been saying, 'What on earth have you got against this man, who has done nothing but go around teaching people about your God? What harm can he possibly have done?'

That same question would have been asked by almost every ordinary Jew. The people whose relatives had been healed by Jesus, the ones who had seen him break bread and feed 5,000 people, the ones who had seen him raise Lazarus from the dead, the ones who had heard his wonderful teaching about God and his kingdom – all of them would have been wondering, 'What is Jesus supposed to have done wrong? We don't understand why you have arrested him!'

In reply to Pilate's question, the Jewish leaders replied, *If he were not a criminal … we would not have handed him over to you* (John 18:30). They knew perfectly well that Jesus had done nothing wrong, so they evaded the question by replying, 'We have brought him here to you, so he must be guilty, mustn't he?' The rights and wrongs of the matter did not interest them; Jesus was a threat to their corrupt power, and so they wanted him to be removed from the scene. That was all there was to it.

Second-hand faith

After speaking with the Jews, Pilate went back into his palace, summoned Jesus and asked him, *Are you the king of the Jews?* (John 18:33). Jesus' reply was remarkable: *Is*

71

that your own idea ... or did the others talk to you about me?
(verse 34). In other words he said, 'What do you think?
I know you have heard me described as the king of the
Jews, I know others have spoken to you about it, but
what do you think about it yourself? What do you really
think about me?'

There is a tendency for some people to know Jesus in
a second-hand way. We may have learned about him
from our Sunday-school teachers, from preachers in
church, from books and so forth, and yet we have only
ever known things *about* Jesus. We have never really
known Jesus himself. We have heard a great deal of
information about him over the years, but we have
never really made it our own, we have never *internalized*
it. Some people find they have a problem when it
comes to witnessing about Jesus, because all they have
to say about him is second-hand; it is all other people's
ideas and experiences. That was the situation in which
Pilate found himself: he had heard about Jesus, but he
didn't know him, and he didn't know what he himself
thought about him.

Luís Palau has made a very significant comment about
this: 'God has no grandchildren.' God has children – that
is, people who believe in Jesus as their personal Saviour –
but he has no grandchildren. We may have grown up in
a Christian family, but the fact that our parents were
committed Christians does not make us Christians. We all
have to make a personal response to Jesus which is ours
and ours alone; no-one else can do this for us. We are
strong, mature Christians precisely in the measure to
which we have personally experienced God for ourselves.
We may have a great deal of knowledge about God and
the Bible; we may be able to quote chapter and verse
from Genesis to Revelation. But the question is, how well
does our faith stand up to the tests which come our way,
such as persecution or sickness or family problems or
other types of suffering? If our faith is only skin-deep, if

our knowledge of God is only in our heads and not in our hearts, then it will be shattered by problems and suffering. Only a real, personal, living relationship with Jesus Christ can survive the storms of life.

We may know all there is to know about the various cuisines of the world; we may know the best items on the menu to order in any restaurant in town. But unless we actually eat the food, it will do us no good. We know all about the food, but unless we digest it we will starve to death! For food to be of any use to us, we must absorb it, we must make it part of ourselves. Similarly, we may know all there is to know about Christianity, but unless we 'digest' it, unless we internalize it, making it real within our hearts and lives, really opening ourselves up to Jesus so that he will come and live within us as our Lord and Saviour in the power of his Holy Spirit, then all our Christian knowledge will be more or less useless to us.

There are some churchgoers who have never really internalized their faith; it has never really penetrated to the very heart of their being. In addition, people who genuinely encountered Jesus for themselves at some stage in the past may come to a point where they cease to internalize the teaching they hear in church. It enters their ears and brains, but never penetrates their hearts. Are we listening to God's Word with our hearts, or with our minds only? I feel that often the preaching in our churches is not sufficiently penetrating. The preachers rush on from one topic to another, assuming that they have really touched us with their message. Instead they need to spend longer on the same subjects until we really receive the message into our hearts, and our lives are permanently changed by it.

The kingdom of God

Jesus told Pilate,

My kingdom is not of this world. If it were, my servants would fight to prevent my arrest by the Jews. But now my kingdom is from another place.

(John 18:36)

I could easily write an entire book about the kingdom of God. It is a vast subject with huge implications for us, and there is a great deal of confusion about it among Christians today. But here and now I can say only a few things about it. It is not a geographical area, like an earthly kingdom or state. It is invisible, but it is nevertheless very real. Literally the Greek phrase means the area or sphere in which God reigns and in which his authority rules. The kingdom of God exists wherever there are people who are under his kingship. It transcends all barriers, whether they be geographical, national, racial, cultural or gender-related.

It also transcends the barrier of time, because it extends from time into eternity. The kingdom of God, unlike the petty kingdoms of humankind, will last for ever. In the history of the world there have been many kingdoms and states, and none of them has lasted for ever. Take, for example, the ancient Persian, Assyrian and Babylonian empires. In their time they were awesomely powerful, but eventually they disintegrated. Think of the empire of Alexander the Great, which extended all the way from Greece to what is now Pakistan. It was an amazing empire while it lasted, but as soon as Alexander died it was divided between his successors. Or take the mighty Roman empire which ruled the whole of the Mediterranean world and even stretched as far north as Hadrian's Wall. It was amazing while it lasted, but it was eventually destroyed by its own evil and overwhelmed by barbarian invaders.

Jesus knew that the Roman empire, while it held the whole of the Western world in thrall during his lifetime, would one day disintegrate and would be outlived by the church which he had founded. He knew that the kingdom of God had already started to grow and would soon expand at an astonishing rate, and that it would outlast all human states. We don't know when Jesus is going to return, but we can be sure of one thing: even if he does not return for many centuries yet, and all the present states of the world disappear and are replaced by other states or super-powers or federations, the kingdom of God will still exist. It is a kingdom which nothing and no-one in the universe can defeat or destroy. It is an eternal, living reality in a world which is dominated by death,

We are citizens of the United Kingdom or of the United States or of whatever country we belong to. That is a fact about us. We may be proud of our nation-ality, or we may be ashamed of the things our country has done and is doing, or we may not feel strongly about it either way. But what is much more important and exciting than our earthly citizenship is the fact that we are part of the kingdom of God and subjects of its King. Our kingdom is never going to fade away, it will never be conquered, it will never do anything we need to be ashamed of, and it will never enter into morally dubious alliances. It is permanent and eternal, it is ruled by the just and righteous God and we are part of it. It amazes me to think that the kingdom which Jesus told Pilate about still exists today and will always exist.

In John 18:37 Pilate says to Jesus, *You are a king, then!* Jesus answers, *You are right in saying I am a king.* Jesus was willing to be identified as the King of the kingdom. While the kingdom itself is invisible, its King is clearly visible. He was born into this world as a human being and lived on this earth for all to see.

Evading Jesus

I believe that Pilate realized that in meeting Jesus he had encountered someone very special. But he avoided facing the truth about him in two ways: by a word and by an action.

First, Jesus said,

For this reason I was born, and for this I came into the world, to testify to the truth. Everyone on the side of truth listens to me.
(John 18:37)

Pilate could then have asked him, 'What do you mean by that?' and Jesus might have replied, 'I am the truth', as he had said back in chapter 14. But instead Pilate asked, *What is truth?* (verse 38). This was not a serious question. Pilate was not asking Jesus to try to reply to this, and Jesus knew it. It was the sort of thing which any well-educated member of the Greek-Roman civilization might have said: it was the kind of intellectual, abstract question which the Greek philosophers liked to ask. One can almost imagine Pilate shrugging his shoulders as he said it. It was simply a throwaway line, designed to deflect the conversation away from the direction it had been taking, which Pilate was finding disturbing.

Many people today ask precisely the same sort of question when confronted by Jesus, the Truth. They ask, 'What is truth?' claiming that no-one can really know what truth is, since everything is relative. Something might be true for you, but it might not be true for me. God is real to you, but not to me. If they don't know what truth is or if there really is such a thing as truth, then they have all the excuse they need to avoid responding to Jesus' claim that he himself was the Truth.

Secondly, Pilate avoided Jesus by an action. Pilate told the Jews,

I find no basis for a charge against him. But it is your custom for me to release to you one prisoner at the time of the Passover. Do you want me to release 'the king of the Jews'?
(John 18:38–39)

But the Jews answered that they wanted the rebel Barabbas instead of Jesus. By this course of action Pilate revealed himself to be a weak, unprincipled man. He knew that Jesus was innocent of any crime, so if he had had any moral backbone, he would have released him and ordered the Jews to leave him alone. He would have had the guts to risk offending the Jewish leaders. He was the governor of Judea, the Emperor's representative, with all the force and authority of the empire behind him and thousands of superbly trained Roman soldiers ready to do his bidding. Yet he told the Jews, 'You yourselves must make the decision; you must decide whether or not Jesus dies.' He refused to take responsibility for his own actions, he refused to wield his power as the governor.

There is some historical evidence that shortly after this, in AD 35, Pilate was recalled to Rome by the Emperor Tiberius, who was very displeased with his performance as governor of Judea. Tiberius died while Pilate was on his way home, so he never was brought to justice, but he may have committed suicide before reaching Rome. There is no evidence that he was an especially evil man; he was probably no worse than most Roman governors, but he was certainly a weak, spineless man.

We should not be too quick to point an accusing finger at Pilate, because in more subtle ways we, too, often try to avoid the force of what Jesus is saying to us. When we hear a sermon, there may be something in it which hits us, and we know that God has spoken to us personally through it. But we don't like what he's saying, because obeying it will be costly and perhaps painful. So a strategy we often use is to pick on some imperfection in the sermon – perhaps the preacher made a factual error or his attitude wasn't quite right in some respect – and we criticize this little thing so that we don't have to think about the important thing which God has said to us through the sermon. This is not unlike Pilate saying, *What is truth?* using a philosophical conundrum to deflect the impact of what Jesus was saying to him. But Jesus is saying to us, 'Don't avoid my Word, because when you accept it and internalize it and make it yours, it will change you and make you more like me, the Son of God.'

Similarly, when God challenges us about something wrong in us, we are quick to blame other people, and to shift the burden of responsibility away from ourselves. 'My parents are to blame, the way they brought me up is to blame, the church is to blame, my school is to blame, society is to blame, my genes are to blame ... Whatever has gone wrong in my life, whatever is wrong with me, it must be someone else's fault – nothing is ever my fault.' Blame-shifting is a popular sport! Pilate washed his hands of the decision about Jesus and handed it over to the Jews, so that if anyone could subsequently be blamed for his death it would be them. We, too, often try to wash our hands of difficult decisions and hand them over to others, so that they can suffer any fallout which may result.

The Jewish leaders chose Barabbas to be released rather than Jesus. It is interesting that this rebel's name, Barabbas, literally means 'son of the father', and it probably indicates that he was the son of a rabbi. Barabbas may have been an example of a good background gone wrong. His attitude might have been, 'Well, I might have turned out all right, but I blame my religious upbringing.' The blame-shifter went free, but the innocent Son of God was led away to be crucified.

Chapter 7

The ultimate choice

Then Pilate took Jesus and had him flogged. The soldiers twisted together a crown of thorns and put it on his head. They clothed him in a purple robe and went up to him again and again, saying, 'Hail, king of the Jews!' And they struck him in the face.

(John 19:1–3)

In legal history there have been many famous trials, but there is none more significant than the trial of Jesus Christ before the Jewish leaders and Pontius Pilate. By modern standards it was an extremely brief trial, lasting thirty-six hours at the most. And yet this trial changed the face of world history and of humanity itself as no other trial had ever done. For this trial led to Jesus' death, and since then the lives of countless billions of Christians all over the world have revolved around the fact that Jesus was born for us, died for us on the cross and rose from the dead three days later. After Jesus' death everything was different; life would not be the same, and neither would death.

The Pilate took Jesus and had him flogged (verse 1). This is a brief sentence, but we should understand what it meant for Jesus. Often people died from a Roman flogging, so severe was the pain and loss of blood and physical strength. Then the Roman soldiers mocked Jesus and beat him up, sarcastically calling him the *king of the Jews* (verse 3).

Children at this time used to play a rather cruel

game with other children who were mentally retarded in some way. They would put a stick in the handicapped child's hand as a sceptre and a paper hat on his head as a crown and would pretend he was a king, marching around him, singing a song of mock adulation and bowing down to him. It seems that the Roman soldiers were playing this game with Jesus. They put a crown of thorns on his head and made him wear a purple robe (the colour purple was symbolic of kingship) and hailed him sarcastically as a king. They thought he was a mere figure of fun, a nobody who had ideas above his station, and so they mocked him just for their own cruel amusement. And yet the immense irony of the situation was that Jesus really was a King – the greatest King who has ever lived or who will ever live, since he was the Son of God. And the soldiers were blinded by their sin and prejudice. Jesus must by now have been weary from lack of sleep, and severely injured by the flogging. They could not see beyond the blood and ripped clothes, they could not see that here was someone of unique stature, the one and only Son of God.

The perfect Lamb of God

Pilate said, *I find no basis for a charge against him* (John 18:38). Now he says the same thing in 19:4, and then again in verse 6. Pilate recognized that Jesus was innocent of any crime. Again, we have a hidden irony in this situation, for what Pilate said was truer than he realized. There was no basis for any accusation of any kind against Jesus, because he was completely and utterly sinless. He was the only person who ever lived who never did anything wrong at all, and that was because he was also God. Even Pilate, although a weak and selfish man, was reluctant to let Jesus be crucified, because he knew he was blameless. If Pilate could have thought of something to charge Jesus with, he would have done so, as it would have eased his conscience and would have pleased the Jewish leadership. But he couldn't find anything in Jesus' conduct to condemn.

Jesus was perfect and totally sinless, and as such he was able to be the sacrifice for our sins. All of us are sinful, and as the penalty for all sin is death, we all deserve to die for our sins. If one of us took it upon himself to die for the sin of humankind, his sacrifice would be useless, because he would simply be dying for his own sin. But since Jesus never, ever sinned, he alone was able to lay down his life as a sacrifice for human-kind, a sacrifice acceptable to God. Because the sinless Jesus died for us, we sinful human beings no longer face the death penalty for our sins, if we put our faith in Jesus as our Saviour. God has taken Jesus' sacrifice and has applied it to every person who has believed in Jesus throughout the centuries, and he will apply it to everyone who believes in him in the future.

What should our response to Jesus be, considering what he has done for us? Immense gratitude and love, of course. How can we ever thank him enough for what he has done for us? The Christian life is not meant to be cold and transactional; it is meant to be relational. We are meant to be in a love relationship with Jesus. Our faith can never be cold and dull if we really understand that Jesus loves us so much that he died for us, and that if you or I had been the only sinful person in the world, he would still have gone to the cross for us. Our faith is meant to be a warm, sincere expression of our love for Jesus, who was absolutely perfect, who did not need to die, and yet who gave up his life for our sakes.

Pilate's declaration that he could find no basis for a charge against Jesus also confirms an important Old Testament principle. In the Old Testament sacrificial system, when a sacrifice was offered for the forgiveness of people's sins, it had to be an animal totally without blemish or defect of any kind. The people had to give their very best animals, not their worst. Similarly, when God made a sacrifice so that the sin of humankind could be forgiven, he gave the very best that he had, and that very best was his one and only Son, Jesus Christ, the spotless, perfect sacrificial Lamb of God. God has given us Jesus, and when we become Christians we receive Jesus and the death he died for us as a gift. God wants us to respond to that with gratitude and love.

When we first become Christians this is all very new and wonderful to us, and our hearts are thrilled by what Jesus has done for us. But once we have been Christians for a while, there is a tendency, if we are not careful, for our initial love for Jesus to grow cold. Our faith loses the vital freshness which it once had. We tend to take Jesus' death for us for granted; it becomes old hat, because we have heard about it so many times before. We lose our amazement at the fact that the perfect Son of God gave his life for someone as sinful as you or I.

'Our minds are made up'

When Jesus came out wearing the crown of thorns and the purple robe, Pilate said to them, 'Here is the man!'

(John 19:5)

This is one of the most famous verses in the Bible, and people have read all sorts of philosophical and theological meanings into it. But I think Pilate, pointing to the weary, bleeding Jesus with his purple robe and crown of thorns, was simply saying, 'Look, here is Jesus, here is the man whom you want crucified, whom you say is a troublemaker and a threat, whom you say is trying to usurp Caesar's rule. Look at him – he is not an impressive figure now. He can be flogged just like anyone else. I don't understand why you want him to be put to death. It is patent nonsense to say he is a rebel against the empire.'

As soon as the chief priests and their officials saw him, they shouted, 'Crucify! Crucify!'

(verse 6)

One might have expected that they would have wanted Pilate to tell them what his conclusions were, having talked with Jesus. What were the facts about Jesus? Did Pilate think he was a threat to the state? But, of course, the Jewish leaders were not remotely interested in the facts about Jesus. They wanted him to be got out of the way. Regardless of whether Jesus had committed a crime, they wanted him to face the death penalty. It was a classic case of 'I have already made up my mind; don't try to confuse me with the facts.'

We too can be guilty of the same mental blindness. We make our minds up about something, and no amount of contrary evidence can lead us to change our point of view. Now, of course, there are some things about which we ought to have a completely inflexible, rigid attitude. For example, I am convinced that Jesus Christ is the Son of God, and I am convinced that he really did rise physically from the dead. I am not prepared to change my mind on either of these things: they are non-negotiable for me.

However, there are a great many things in life about which our views need to be open to change. Very often we have to make judgments about things or people when we are not in possession of the full facts, and we have to come to a provisional decision about them, recognizing that if we learn some more facts about the matter, we may need to modify our point of view. But very often we take up rigid attitudes when we should have flexible ones. We hear or see something about a particular person which seems to cast a dubious light on her character or behaviour, and so we place that person in our mental pigeon-hole marked 'no good'. We have made up our minds about her, and if we subsequently learn something good about her, we ignore it, because it doesn't accord with our first judgment about her.

The same situation holds with attitudes we may have had for a long time about the church or about life in general. Later in life we may see evidence that those attitudes are wrong or at least inaccurate, but we refuse to change our views because our minds are closed. It is very dangerous to have a closed mind, because it means we cannot hear the voice of God, and if we cannot hear his voice we are bound to make some serious mistakes in our lives. We need to be open-minded in our relationships with one another and in our learning and growing, but this open-mindedness also needs to be based on the non-negotiable facts of the Christian faith.

Committed to the truth?

In John 19:7 we once again see Jesus' enemies unwittingly speaking the truth about him:

The Jews insisted, 'We have a law, and according to that law he must die, because he claimed to be the Son of God.'

They thought Jesus had blasphemed by claiming to be God's Son and therefore deserved to die, but in fact he really was God's Son, and he had come into the world to die for the sin of humankind.

When Pilate heard this, he was even more afraid, and he went back inside the palace. 'Where do you come from?' he asked Jesus, but Jesus gave him no answer.

(verses 8–9)

Jesus had refused to answer the Jewish leaders' questions, and now he refused to answer those of Pilate. This was a fulfilment of the prophecy in Isaiah 53:7:

He was oppressed and afflicted, yet he did not open his mouth; he was led like a lamb to the slaughter, and as a sheep before her shearers is silent, so he did not open his mouth.

Also, Jesus knew that there was no point in answering any questions, because no-one involved wanted to know the truth about him. The Jewish leaders wanted him out of the way because he threatened their power over the people. Pilate wanted to please both the Jews and the Emperor at the same time, whatever the truth or untruth of the charges against Jesus. We read in Luke 23 that Jesus was also brought before King Herod, who happened to be in Jerusalem at that time. But he was interested only in seeing Jesus do a miracle and in protecting his own position, so Jesus refused to answer his questions too. All these people were merely looking out for their own vested interests and were not in the least bit interested in the truth about Jesus.

It has to be said that many Christians are not as committed to truth as they should be. They are more interested in having their needs met, and in having their problems solved, than in what God is saying. I have frequently encountered gross hypocrisy among Christians. They may say, 'Oh yes, we believe that the Bible is the Word of God and we ought to obey it,' but as soon as problems come, as soon as it costs them something to obey the Word, then they throw their Christian principles out of the window and say, 'Well, obviously, the Bible doesn't quite mean what it says; God can't possibly want me to do X or to stop doing Y, because I don't want to do X and I don't want to stop doing Y.'

We are very good at condemning other people's sins, aren't we? Most of us read our Bibles and notice the sins which are the least bothersome to us personally. We are scarcely tempted by those sins at all, and so we are very keen to spot them in other people's lives. We are not likely to commit those sins, and so we can condemn them with ease, whereas we tend to play down the parts of Scripture which refer to the sins which do bother us. 'Well, of course,' we say, 'the Bible appears to condemn this sin, but does it really? And anyway, it isn't anywhere near as serious a sin as sins *A* and *B*, which those other people commit.' For example, the Bible condemns gossiping. Someone may be a compulsive gossip, always tearing people apart when they're not in the room. 'But I'm not really gossipping,' he says, 'I am merely sharing my concern about this person with a third party ... and a fourth and a fifth ...'

It is amazing how hard some Christians will try to avoid facing up to what God's Word is saying to them. I have heard people try to justify the most obvious sins, such as stealing from their employer, or adultery, or blatant lying, or cynical manipulation of other people. I have known Christians who have searched the Scriptures trying to find justification for behaviour which is clearly sinful. They care more about expediency than truth. When it comes to the crunch, they will take the easy way out rather than have to suffer, even just a little, for the sake of truth and obedience to God. Some of the worst pastoral problems in any church are caused by people's willingness to dilute God's truth, and to make it less potent so that they can get away with a lifestyle which is inferior to the true one which Jesus wants of us. Sometimes when we pray, heaven seems to be as silent as stone, and often the reason for this is that our motivation is wrong; we are merely trying to protect our own skins and are not interested in being obedient to God.

The real men and women of God, the people who will leave a permanent and godly mark on this generation, are the people whose lives are bound to God's truth rather than to their own interests, people who stick to their principles even when it costs them something.

Tapping into the real Power

When Jesus remained silent, Pilate said,

'Do you refuse to speak to me? … Don't you realise I have the power either to free you or to crucify you?'

Jesus answered, 'You would have no power over me if it were not given to you from above.'

(John 19:10–11)

Jesus was saying that Pilate's power was given to him by God; in itself Pilate's power was puny, a mere nothing compared to the power of the Son of God.

Here is an analogy to help us understand the situation. An ant is walking up the road, but its way is blocked by an elephant. The ant says, 'Get out of my way!'

The elephant just ignores it. Then the ant says, 'Do you know who I am? I'm the King of the Ants! So you had better get out of my way!'

Then the elephant, irritated by the ant, gently raises one foot and squashes the ant.

Pilate is like the King of the Ants. He says to Jesus, 'Don't you know who I am? I'm a very important man! I'm the governor of Judea!'

And Jesus, knowing that Pilate is a mere nothing, answers, 'The only power you have over me is the power which my Father has given you.'

Going back to the ant and elephant analogy, it is as if the elephant said to the ant, 'All right, I'll get out of your way, but only because my father has told me to do so.'

The situation was deeply ironic; there was Jesus, the greatest power in the world, through whom the universe had been formed in the beginning, placed in the hands of this puppet figure, Pilate, in order that the kingdom of God might come into the world through his death and resurrection.

All power comes from God; he is the real source of power. Pilate had power over Jesus only because God had given it to him. The greatest power in the universe is not gravity or the nuclear fusion going on in the hearts of stars, but the power of the Creator. The greatest power in human affairs is not the political power of kings and emperors and presidents and prime ministers, or the economic power of the great multinational corporations, or the ideological power of religious and political creeds. It is the power of God. If we, the church, really want to influence the world we are living in, we need to tap into the power of God. God is the one who has the real and ultimate authority, and if we are acting in his name and doing his will, there is no power on earth which can stand against us. God's power runs the world, and one day his Son is going to come back to claim the world for himself. God is running things according to his own timetable and he is doing his own thing, and we need to get into step with what he is doing. One day all the world will bow the knee to Jesus Christ, and all other powers will be abolished.

The slippery slope of compromise

From then on, Pilate tried to set Jesus free, but the Jews kept shouting, 'If you let this man go, you are no friend of Caesar. Anyone who claims to be a king opposes Caesar.'

(John 19:12)

Finally they said, *We have no king but Caesar* (verse 15). This was a remarkable turnaround! The Jews hated Caesar, because he claimed to be a god and demanded their worship, and they would worship only their own God. And yet now they were so determined to get rid of Jesus that they were even willing to acknowledge Caesar as their king. They had come to the point where they had made the final choice: the choice between Jesus and the Emperor.

How had they come to this position? By making many small choices against Jesus, they had finally come to make the ultimate choice. Time after time they saw him do something of which they disapproved, and each time their hostility to him increased. At first they were angry, then they became resentful, then they became bitter, then they schemed to have him killed, and then they arrested him and let their prejudice blind them to the truth about him, and now, at last, they chose Caesar instead of Jesus.

A similar principle is at work in some Christians today. Some people make a decision to follow Jesus and they come into the life of the church, and everything is apparently okay. They say and do the things which Christians are expected to say and do. But in their hearts they are continuously making little choices against Jesus, compromising their faith in many minor ways. They are choosing to go back into the world; they are choosing the enemy's values rather than God's; expediency rather than truth. Then eventually all those little choices against Jesus add up to the big choice of turning away from the living God and to the devil and his kingdom.

In any church there will be people who are already on the slippery slope of compromise; they have made the wrong choice so many times that they are in danger of choosing the god of this world instead of Jesus. On Sundays they go to church and claim that Jesus is Lord, but from Monday to Saturday their commitment to him is so drastically compromised that they hardly have a relationship with him at all and are beginning to serve a different master. With their lips they say they serve Jesus, but in their hearts they serve another lord.

All Christians need to watch their own hearts for

evidence of this compromise which in the end leads to a rejection of God. We need constantly to walk close to Jesus, and to make him the Lord of our lives in all the real, practical choices which we have to make.

Chapter 8

The crucified King

Finally Pilate handed him over to them to be crucified.

So the soldiers took charge of Jesus. Carrying his own cross, he went out to the place of the Skull (which in Aramaic is called Golgotha). Here they crucified him, and with him two others – one on each side and Jesus in the middle.

Pilate had a notice prepared and fastened to the cross. It read: JESUS OF NAZARETH, THE KING OF THE JEWS. Many of the Jews read this sign, for the place where Jesus was crucified was near the city, and the sign was written in Aramaic, Latin and Greek. The chief priests of the Jews protested to Pilate, 'Do not write "The King of the Jews," but that this man claimed to be king of the Jews.'

Pilate answered, 'What I have written, I have written.'

(John 19:16–22)

The Jewish leaders thought that Jesus' claim to be the King of the Jews was a false one, and so they pressurized Pilate into having him crucified. Jesus also claimed to be God, and the Son of God, and the Messiah. He also called himself the Way, the Truth and the Life, and the Light of the World, and the Bread of Life. He told the people that if they believed in him, they would have eternal life. Jesus made some truly amazing claims about himself, and the Jewish leaders rejected all of them. Similarly, everyone today has to make a decision about the claims which Jesus made about himself. To say that he was merely a good man and nothing more is nonsense. Would someone who was merely a good man have claimed that he was God and that he personally could provide eternal life for everyone who believed in him? As C. S. Lewis so clearly argued, we all have to decide between three views of Jesus. We can decide that the things he said were untrue and that he knew they were untrue, which means that he cannot have been a good man, but a deceiver. Or we can decide that they were untrue but he believed they were true, which means that he was deluded. Or we can decide that the things he said really were true, which means that we must take them seriously. In other words, Jesus was either bad, or mad, or God. There is no way we can say he was merely a good man, for no mere good man would have claimed to be God.

Those of us who have been Christians for a long time need to understand just how shocking Jesus' claims about himself were. We are so used to hearing them that they seem commonplace to us. But Jesus' claims were the most dynamic, stupendous claims ever made by any person who ever lived on earth. There have been many brilliant scientists through the centuries who have made staggering claims about their discoveries, but none has ever made a claim as amazing as this one:

I am the resurrection and the life. He who believes in me will live, even though he dies; and whoever lives and believes in me will never die.

(John 11:25–26)

Every person alive today must make a decision about Jesus, as the Jewish leaders had to. Is he the Son of God or isn't he? If he isn't, then really Christianity is a waste of time. If Jesus didn't die on the cross as God's perfect sacrifice for our sins, and if he didn't really rise from the dead so that we too might have victory over death, then there is no point in being a Christian. Christianity would be just a lot of useless words with no substance.

We might just as well all be humanists or hedonists and do whatever seems best to us. But if Jesus really was God, then we must believe in him as our Saviour with all our hearts. We must totally give our lives over to his lordship, and we must bow down to him in adoration and praise. Have you decided about Jesus yet?

Jesus the great High Priest

When the soldiers crucified Jesus, they took his clothes, dividing them into four shares, one for each of them, with the undergarment remaining. This garment was seamless, woven in one piece from top to bottom.

'Let's not tear it,' they said to one another. 'Let's decide by lot who will get it.'

This happened that the scripture might be fulfilled which said,

> *'They divided my garments among them*
> *and cast lots for my clothing.'*

So this is what the soldiers did.

(John 19:23–24)

The Jewish high priests used to wear a seamless garment, and its purpose was to symbolize the oneness of the Jewish people under God, and the high priest's role as the person who brought God and the people together as one. The fact that Jesus wore this seamless garment, then, means that he was a high priest – the final and greatest High Priest, after whom no others would be needed. Jesus was the High Priest who on the cross bridged the chasm of sin between God and humankind, holding God with one hand and humankind with the other, and made it possible for God and people to know each other.

Near the cross of Jesus stood his mother, his mother's sister, Mary the wife of Clopas, and Mary of Magdala.

(John 19:25)

It took courage for them to do this, for by being so near to Jesus' cross they were identifying themselves with him and thereby exposing themselves to the hostility of the Jewish and Roman authorities. And yet they were there because they had been drawn by their love for Jesus. Mary his mother loved him as only a mother can love her son; she wanted to be near him at his dying moment. She was prepared to face personal risk to be there with him at his hour of greatest need. The other women were there because Jesus had helped them and they believed in him as the Messiah.

The willingness of these women to face danger because of their love for Jesus is a challenge to all of us. All Christians have so much to thank Jesus for; we should all be there at the foot of the cross, witnessing to Jesus, taking the risk of being identified as followers of Jesus. And yet many of us who have been Christians for some years are riddled with ingratitude. We take Jesus for granted; we have become almost casual about our relationship with him; our faith has lost the freshness and vitality which it once had. Let us ask God to make Jesus' sacrifice of himself for us real and alive to us once again.

When Jesus saw his mother there, and the disciple whom he loved (probably John) *standing near by, he said to his mother, 'Dear woman, here is your son,' and to the disciple, 'Here is your mother.' From that time on, this disciple took her into his home.*

(John 19:26–27)

The Greek term rendered *dear woman* in the NIV is hard to translate, but in the context of a family home it really means something as intimate as 'dear Mum'. Joseph was probably dead by now, and so Jesus was concerned that Mary would have trouble getting by without her eldest son. Looking down on her from the cross, he was saying to her, 'Dear Mum, I love you and I know you love me, and I appreciate all that you have done for me throughout my life. I am dying now, but I want you to be cared for in your old age. John here will take you home and care for you as if you were his own mother. And Mum, I want you to care for John and help him just as you have helped me all these years.'

It is astonishing that at this time, when Jesus was enduring the terrible physical agony of the cross and was just a very short time away from his death, he was more concerned about others than himself. He was still thinking about his mother and his beloved friend John, wanting to make sure that they would be all right after he was no longer with them in the flesh. I long for that selflessness, for the spiritual maturity to be more concerned about others than myself, no matter how difficult the circumstances of my own life may happen to be. Many of us are good at caring for other people so long as everything is going well for us, but when we are up against problems, when we have been hurt in some way, when we are going through pressure or stress, our caring ceases, and those we had cared for are left to fend for themselves. Some Christians are years away from that attitude on the road of spiritual maturity.

'It is finished'

Later, knowing that all was now completed, and so that the Scripture would be fulfilled, Jesus said, 'I am thirsty.' A jar of wine vinegar was there, so they soaked a sponge in it, put the sponge on a stalk of the hyssop plant, and lifted it to Jesus' lips. When he had received the drink, Jesus said, 'It is finished.' With that, he bowed his head and gave up his spirit.

(John 19:28–30)

We should not think that because Jesus was the Son of God, his suffering on the cross was less than that of any other crucified man. His death was a fully human one, full of pain and suffering. God didn't take away any of the pain for him; he truly suffered on the cross for you and me.

The words translated *It is finished* are actually a phrase used by the people of the time to conclude business transactions. When a deal was agreed, the two parties would say this. Jesus was not saying in despair, 'I am finished', but rather, 'The work which I came to earth to do is finished. I have died a sacrificial death for humankind, so that all who believe in me may be saved in me. I have defeated the kingdom of darkness. I have lived a perfect life, as I had to do to be God's sacrificial Lamb. I have resisted the temptations of the devil. I have obeyed my heavenly Father in every way.' Jesus' words here were actually a cry of victory, not of defeat. It was indeed finished; Jesus won salvation for us, and there is nothing that any of us can do to add to what he has done, because he has done everything necessary for us. We do not need to work for our salvation, because Jesus has bought it for us with his own life; all we need to do is to have faith in him.

The Greek phrase which the NIV translates as *he bowed his head and gave up his spirit* has the sense of Jesus handing his life over to someone else, to God. The implication is that no-one *took* Jesus' life; he *gave* his life for us, deliberately and willingly. John 3:16 tells us that *God so loved the world that he gave his one and only Son.* Since the Father had already given Jesus, he, always wanting to obey his Father, willingly gave himself. Jesus was not robbed of his life by wicked people; he gave his life to God as the final, ultimate expression of his total dedication and obedience to God.

John saw it all

John 19:31 tells us that *it was the day of Preparation* – that is, for the Sabbath, which was the next day. And it was a very special Sabbath. It was the feast of the Passover, when the Jews celebrated the fact that during their nation's enslavement in Egypt, death had passed over them because of the blood of the sacrificial lambs which had been daubed on the doorposts of their houses. All the firstborn of the Egyptians died that night, but the Jews were untouched by the plague of death. The Old Testament law forbade an execution on the Sabbath, so the Jews wanted to get the bodies of the three crucified men off the crosses and neatly disposed of beforehand, especially since this was the Passover and not just an ordinary Sabbath.

So *they asked Pilate to have the legs broken and the bodies taken down* (verse 31). When a crucified man was taking too long to die, his death was sometimes speeded up by breaking his legs. This was not a clean, merciful, surgical procedure; rather, the Roman soldiers would take large mallets and smash the legs until the man died from shock, pain and loss of blood. The full weight of his body would hang from his arms and death would have been accelerated by suffocation. (This should serve to dispel any illusion we may have about what sort of death crucifixion was; it was an appallingly barbaric way to execute someone, and involved excruciating, protracted pain.)

So the soldiers came and broke the legs of the two men who had been crucified with Jesus. They found that Jesus was already dead, so they did not bother to break his legs. Instead, just to make completely sure that Jesus was dead, one of the soldiers pierced Jesus' side with a spear, and the result was *a sudden flow of blood and water* (verse 34).

Roman soldiers were highly efficient and ruthless professional killers; when they set out to kill someone, they made a thorough job of it. The fact that a soldier put a spear in Jesus' side is a sure guarantee that when he was put in the tomb he really was completely dead.

It would not have been a mere superficial wound. The spear would have been thrust in deep – deep enough to have killed even someone who had not already suffered serious blood loss and endured hours nailed to a cross. So it is absurd for anyone to suggest that the resurrection was a sham because Jesus never really died. The idea is that Jesus was taken down from the cross before he had died and was put in a tomb. In that cool environment he recovered from his injuries, stripped off all his burial cloths and left the tomb, somehow managing to remove the huge boulder which had sealed the entrance. What nonsense!

Why was there a *sudden flow of blood and water* when Jesus' side was pierced with the spear? I believe that the water and blood were a sign pointing to the Lord's Supper and to baptism in water. Just in case anyone might be tempted to doubt this part of his account, John here adds the declaration,

The man who saw it has given testimony, and his testimony is true.

(John 19:35)

John is referring to himself; he is reminding us that he has written an eye-witness account; he is recording what he saw himself.

Why did he record it? John *knows that he tells the truth, and he testifies so that you also may believe* (verse 35). He did not write so that people could discuss whether or not these things happened, but so that people would believe in Jesus as the Saviour.

Finally, John comments that

These things happened so that the scripture would be fulfilled, 'Not one of his bones will be broken,' and, as another scripture says, 'They will look on the one they have pierced.'

(verses 36–37)

Writing with hindsight some years later, John understood that in every way Jesus' death on the cross was a fulfilment of many prophecies in the Old Testament (see Exodus 12:46; Numbers 9:12; Psalm 34:20 and Zechariah 12:10).

When we are witnessing to our faith in Jesus we need to remember that it is not based on myth or fable; it is based on accurate historical accounts. Our faith is founded on actual events which happened at the beginning of the first century AD. We believe in Jesus Christ, who was a real person who existed in real history in a real place, Palestine. The Gospels are full of known figures like Pontius Pilate, about whom there are historical records other than the New Testament. The Gospels are reliable history. What is more, in the case of John's Gospel we have the account of someone who actually saw these things happen. He really was there when Jesus died on the cross, and he recorded what he saw. John was not writing fiction for our entertainment. Fiction such as we have in the modern novel, where imaginary characters act out an imaginary story, did not exist in the ancient world. John was recording actual events which he personally witnessed.

Some Christians are defensive about the Bible; they fear that its critics will pull it apart. But we don't need to be defensive. It contains sixty-six books written by about forty different authors in three languages over a span of thousands of years. Today thousands of texts and fragments of texts of the biblical books still exist, and some of those texts are almost as old as Christianity itself. We know that the Bible which we read today is the same Bible which the early church compiled. By comparison, the *Book of Mormon* has been in existence for only about 200 years, and yet in that time it has received about 3,000 major alterations. We don't need to defend the Bible: that would be just as pointless as trying to defend an angry tiger. What we need to do is let the Bible out of its cage and do its work in the world because it is the Word of God, full of God's power. The Bible is a sure foundation for our Christian lives, and it demands our trust and commitment too.

Secret disciples

> *Later, Joseph of Arimathea asked Pilate for the body of Jesus. Now Joseph was a disciple of Jesus, but secretly because he feared the Jews. With Pilate's permission, he came and took the body. He was accompanied by Nicodemus, the man who earlier had visited Jesus at night.*

> (John 19:38–39)

Both Joseph and Nicodemus were members of the Sanhedrin, the Jewish ruling council. They had probably lain low while the Sanhedrin had secured the execution of Jesus, since they had no wish to be party to his death but also were afraid to defend him publicly. They were secret disciples while he was alive, and now that he was dead they wanted to do what they could for him to show their commitment to him.

Many Christians are secret disciples of Jesus. If some of our neighbours or workmates were to turn up at our churches one Sunday morning, would they be surprised to meet us there, since they had no idea that we were Christians? I have to confess that at times in my life I have been a secret disciple. When I was at school doing my 'A' Levels I was the chairman of the Christian Union, and I found it easy to talk about the Lord with my Christian friends. But my witnessing to other people in the school was almost non-existent. One of my fellow sixth-formers became a Christian at an evangelistic meeting and she came and told me about it. 'That's really great,' I said.

Then she explained that a Christian at the meeting who knew me had told her to tell me about her new commitment to Jesus, since I was a Christian too. 'But

how come I never knew you were a Christian before?'
she asked me.

I was ashamed at this question. I had known this girl
quite well for some time, but somehow she had never
noticed my Christian faith, because it had been almost
invisible. I still find that a painful memory.

It is easy to speak to our fellow Christians about
Jesus, but it is another thing to witness to people who
are indifferent or even hostile to the Christian
message. In those circumstances it is much easier to
keep quiet about our faith, and this is what great
numbers of Christians do much of the time. Some of us
can be outrageously Christian at church on a Sunday
morning, full of joy and praise to God, but on a
Monday morning we become completely different. We
lead a kind of Jeckyll and Hyde existence: we have a
Sunday personality and a very different Monday-to-
Saturday personality. We may speak boldly about our
faith on Sunday, but on Monday morning we are
somehow struck dumb. Now, I don't say that to get at
other people, because I have experienced this problem
myself. These days I find it much easier to witness
about Jesus, but I do sympathize with secret disciples.

Some people make a commitment to Jesus but are
too afraid to tell anyone – even other Christians. I
would like to encourage secret disciples to come out of
the closet. Tell people in the church you go to, tell your
husband or wife, tell your children, tell your
workmates. Tell them that you know and love Jesus,
and ask him for strength to talk to others about him.

A King's burial

*Nicodemus brought a mixture of myrrh and aloes, about
seventy-five pounds. Taking Jesus' body, the two of them
wrapped it, with the spices, in strips of linen. This was
in accordance with Jewish burial customs.*

(John 19:39–40)

101

Seventy-five pounds (about 34 kilos) of very expensive spice was far more than an ordinary burial would have required. This was a special burial, a burial fit for royalty. Joseph and Nicodemus recognized that Jesus was a King, and so they were trying to give him a fitting burial, as a sign of their love and respect for him.

At the place where Jesus was crucified, there was a garden, and in the garden a new tomb, in which no-one had ever been laid.
(verse 41)

There is great significance in the fact that Jesus' tomb was a brand new one. There was something new, fresh, different and world-shaking about the death of Jesus, because it was to be followed by resurrection. This was a unique event in history, after which death and life would never be the same again. In the death of Jesus God was doing something totally new which would transform human history.

Because it was the Jewish day of Preparation and since the tomb was near by, they laid Jesus there.
(verse 42)

But this was a preparation not just for the Jewish feast of Passover, but for a whole new way of life. Jesus had been born into the world, had lived his perfectly sinless life and had died as the sacrifice for our sins. Now there would be a brief wait for three days, after which Jesus would rise from the dead and the new dimension of resurrection life in Jesus would be opened up to humanity. Jesus' whole life of thirty-three years had a been a preparation for his death and resurrection, since to die for our sins had been the reason for his incarnation as a human being. His whole life had been leading up to this, and through his resurrection the history of the world was going to be the most important event in the history of humankind.

People who are not Christians have not yet tapped

into the significance of that great event. They are, as it were, merely observing it from a distance, from the outside. But once we are Christians we are on the inside of that event. We are not literally transported back in time to first-century Palestine, but spiritually we become part of what happened then. We are in Christ, and so we are resurrected from death with him. Until a person becomes a Christian, he or she is missing out on the greatest event in history. Don't miss out. Get on the inside of the action!

If we are already Christians, we need to get excited and to stay excited about the resurrection. We have experienced its reality in our own lives. Jesus Christ was raised from the dead by God, and we too have shared in his resurrection by faith in him. We can truly say, 'I was there!'

Chapter 9

Jesus is alive!

Early on the first day of the week, while it was still dark, Mary Magdalene went to the tomb and saw that the stone had been removed from the entrance. So she came running to Simon Peter and the other disciple, the one Jesus loved, and said, 'They have taken the Lord out of the tomb, and we don't know where they have put him!'

(John 20:1–2)

The resurrection of Jesus from death is unique in the history of the world: he is the only person who was ever resurrected. In history quite a few people have been *resuscitated*, but only Jesus has been *resurrected*. For example, Jesus' friend Lazarus died and was sealed up in his tomb, and Jesus raised him from death. There is no doubt that he was really dead and that Jesus really brought him back to life; he was not in a coma. In Luke 7 we read that Jesus raised to life the dead son of the widow of Nain. Since the foundation of the church many people have been raised from death. Quite a few cases of this have been reported in recent years. However, these were cases of resuscitation, not resurrection. All these people died and were raised from death by the power of Jesus, but one day, having lived out a normal life-span, they all died once more. Jesus, however, was raised from the dead by God and will *never* die again. In the case of the other people, the victory over death was only temporary; in the case of Jesus, death was defeated *permanently*. He rose from the dead never to die again. Because Christians are in Christ Jesus, they share in his total and eternal victory over death and have eternal life in him.

John's account of the disciples discovering that Jesus' tomb was empty is amazingly fresh and real. It is obvious that it was written by someone who was actually there. There are little details, such as John getting to the tomb before Peter, peering into the tomb and seeing the strips of burial linen. The resurrection was not a mere piece of wishful thinking by the disciples. It took them completely by surprise; it really happened. Christians can be assured that their faith is based on a real event for which there is solid evidence. We don't need to be frightened of what the world will think when we talk about our faith. I would love Christians to be much more positive and robust in talking about Jesus. We should not be amazed of our faith, thinking that the world has all the answers and we are somehow behind the times and vulnerable to criticism.

There are some remarkable double standards at work in our society. People write off the resurrection of Jesus as first-century mass hysteria, and yet they readily believe the nonsense which some modern scientists and philosophers peddle. Of course, a classic example of scientific wishful thinking is found where there is blind faith in the theory of Evolution by natural selection. Now, of course, it is obvious that evolution happens, as it can be observed in the development of species today. However, that does not mean that species have developed by a blind, random process through the survival of the fittest. Darwin always acknowledged that his theory was precisely that – a theory – and hoped that in years to come science would provide evidence to substantiate it. But that evidence has never really materialized, and today some scientists are saying that in order to explain the development of species it is necessary to theorize the operation of some kind of directing, purposive force which guides evolution. (Christians call this force God!) And yet, despite the lack of evidence for aspects of evolution, generations of people have believed it because 'science' has told them to. The modern 'cult of science' has a great deal to answer for; it has warped people's minds and prejudiced them against the gospel. The people of the Western world have been conned into believing in a religion of science, thinking it has proved things which it hasn't even begun to explain.

By contrast, we have plenty of evidence for believing in the resurrection. Now, of course, the resurrection is still something which requires faith. It can't be real and life-changing to us unless we believe. But, on the other hand, what is required is not a blind faith – a leap into the dark – but faith in something for which there is solid evidence.

Mary's love for Jesus

John 20:1 tells us that the first person to discover that the tomb was empty was Mary Magdalene, and she was also the first person to see the risen Jesus. Actually the word translated *early* literally means the last watch of the night, that is, between 3 am and 6 am. In other words, she was so distressed about Jesus dying that she went to the tomb even in the night.

I believe that she was given the privilege of seeing Jesus before anyone else because, of all his disciples, she was the most grateful. She had been demon-possessed and Jesus had cast the evil spirits out of her. There is also some evidence both in Scripture and elsewhere that she was a prostitute. Jesus had liberated her from demonic oppression and had lifted her out of moral bondage, and he had set her life upon a safe, strong foundation – that is, himself. The other disciples were, by the standards of their culture, not bad people. Peter and Andrew were honest, hard-working fishermen. Jesus did not lift them out of the gutter. Mary, however, would have been one of the outcasts of Jewish society, despised and shunned by all 'respectable' Jews. But Jesus had delivered her from evil and had treated her with respect and love; no-one else had ever treated her that way before.

And so she felt devastated that Jesus had been killed. She felt she had to be near to him, even though he was dead. Perhaps she was even hoping against hope that somehow he would still be alive, so distraught was she at losing the only person who really meant anything to her.

I long that I and all Christians would have the sort of love for Jesus which Mary Magdalene had – a love which is full of gratitude to him and a recognition of all he has done for us. In a sense it is more difficult for people who have grown up in Christian homes to have that sort of love for Jesus than it is for people who have been converted from pagan backgrounds. Now, of course, we should be grateful for our Christian up-bringing, because it saves us from much of the pain and suffering which people from pagan homes experience and it teaches us about the Lord from an early age. But there is a tendency for us simply to slide into being Christians. We may not be able to remember clearly when we gave our lives to Jesus. It may well have been when we were five or six. We had good moral and spiritual teaching from our parents and churches when we were children, and so we never became involved in anything which was obviously sinful, such as crime or drugs or casual sex. Our conversion was real, since all people – even the children of Christian parents – are born sinful and need Jesus as their Saviour to save them from their sin. But for us there was no marked transformation from a life of sinful degradation to a holy, God-pleasing life, since we were taught by our parents to lead good lives. Consequently it is more difficult for us to relate to someone like Mary, who was dramatically transformed by Jesus. People who are converted from a thoroughly pagan background find it easier to understand her, since they can clearly remember leading a dissolute life and then being turned around by Jesus.

My prayer is that all Christians, whatever their background, will love Jesus as Mary did, with a passionate, grateful love. I pray that those of us who grew up in Christian homes will be able to recognize what kind of people we would have become if we had not had such a good upbringing. Our attitude should not be 'holier than thou' but 'There but for the grace of God go I'. Without Jesus and the example of our parents we could have ended up in all sorts of trouble and degradation. We have been protected and delivered by Jesus from a great deal of evil. I pray that our faith will be full of gratitude to him for dying for us so that we could be free from evil and forgiven of our sin. Because Jesus has taken hold of us, we are far, far better people than we would otherwise have been. I long that that sense of gratitude to Jesus will permeate our lives and express itself in wholehearted commitment to him and in heartfelt worship.

Seeing and believing

So she came running to Simon Peter (John 20:2). Why did Mary run to Peter with the news that the tomb had been opened? Because everyone recognized that Peter was still the leader, despite the fact that he had denied Jesus three times. Jesus had clearly marked Peter as the leader, and all the disciples respected him because of that.

So Peter and the other disciple started for the tomb. Both were running, but the other disciple outran Peter and reached the tomb first.

(verse 3)

John probably got there first because he was younger and fitter than Peter. But John didn't step right into the tomb when he got there; he looked into it, but waited for Peter to go in first, since Peter was the leader.

Finally the other disciple, who had reached the tomb first, also went inside. He saw and believed.

(verse 8)

In other words, John saw the strips of linen and the folded burial cloth and knew that Jesus had risen from the dead. And suddenly he had a blinding flash of understanding. Now he understood what Jesus had been talking about when he had said that the Jews could destroy this temple, but in three days it would be back again (see John 2:19). Jesus really had meant that he would literally die and literally rise from the dead. Suddenly John saw everything Jesus had said in a new light of understanding.

Referring to the other disciples, John writes,

They still did not understand from Scripture that Jesus had to rise from the dead.

(verse 9)

Jesus must sometimes have felt very frustrated with the disciples. He spelled things out to them again and again, but the message just didn't seem to get through their thick skulls. So when it came to his death, they thought that that was it; Jesus' influence was finished, and they would never see him again – despite the fact that he had told them that he would rise from the dead. Only when the resurrection actually happened did they understand what he had said.

Some Christian leaders have a similar experience. They try for month after month, year after year, to lead their people into a closer, more dynamic relationship with Jesus, and it seems that they are wasting their breath. After months of teaching, someone at a meeting may say something which shows that he has completely failed to grasp what the leader has been driving at for all this time. The leader has been trying to lead the people to be the resurrection people of God, filled with the Holy Spirit's power and love. Yet they seem to think that all God wants them to do is to carry on being good Baptists or Anglicans or Methodists or whatever they are, keeping the time-honoured denominational tread-mill turning smoothly. The leader feels that he would get the same results if he simply went and banged his head against a brick wall; it wouldn't be any more painful, and it would certainly consume less time and energy! But the marvellous thing is that Jesus had to cope with disciples like that too, and in the end God was able to work through them in an amazing way. So leaders today can hope that their efforts too will in the end produce results. Frankly, the only thing which will wake up some church members is seeing the power of God as John did in the empty tomb and having their understanding transformed by it.

Angels in white

> Then the disciples went back to their homes, but Mary stood outside the tomb crying. As she wept, she bent over to look into the tomb and saw two angels in white, seated where Jesus' body had been, one at the head and the other at the foot.
>
> They asked her, 'Woman, why are you crying?'
>
> 'They have taken my Lord away,' she said, 'and I don't know where they have put him.'

(John 20:10–13)

Mary was crying because she was in deep distress. Jesus was the only man who had ever truly loved her and respected her, and who had looked at her without lust. She thought she had seen the last of him. She was bitterly upset and afraid. But look at verse 14:

110

At this, she turned round and saw Jesus standing there, but she did not realise that it was Jesus.

Her problem was that she was facing in the wrong direction. She was looking into the tomb, but Jesus was right behind her. When we are upset or anxious or weighed down with problems, many of us look in the wrong direction for help. Instead of looking towards Jesus, we look into ourselves, into our own resources; or we look to other people; or we look for help in books. Some people seek shelter in frantic activity: when they have problems they make themselves very busy, so that they never have time to stop and think, because thinking makes them depressed or anxious.

Jesus said to Mary,

'Woman ... why are you crying? Who is it you are looking for?'

(verse 15)

The translation 'woman' is misleading; the word in the original language is much gentler than that.

Thinking he was the gardener, she said, 'Sir, if you have carried him away, tell me where you have put him, and I will get him.'

(verse 15)

Mary was desperate to see Jesus again, but she didn't really believe that she would see him. Her eyes were full of tears and her head was probably bowed down, so she couldn't see him. She just heard a voice, which she mistook for the gardener's. She couldn't believe that her wildest dreams had come true, that Jesus was alive after all.

Jesus said to her, 'Mary.'

She turned towards him and cried out in Aramaic, 'Rabboni!' (which means Teacher).

(verse 16)

111

This is one of the most poignant and moving verses in John's Gospel. Jesus made contact with her simply by saying her name, and so she recognized him, calling him 'Rabboni!' This literally means 'Teacher' but also means 'Father, Lord, Master, Friend'. When all seems lost, when we are in despair, sometimes Jesus will come to us and speak to us by name – perhaps not audibly, but we know that he has come close to us personally. It might be in a church service or a home group or just when we are praying privately. Suddenly we know that Jesus has spoken to us; something clicks within us, and we are never the same again. That was how it was for Mary. Suddenly she knew that Jesus was still with her, that he knew her personally, that he was alive, and that therefore everything else in her life could be coped with.

When young children are ill they suffer more than adults because they don't have the experience to know that they are ill and that the illness will eventually pass and they will feel well again. All they know is that they feel awful and they think it's going to go on that way permanently. It is a comfort to the child if Mum or Dad comes and gives them a cuddle. It doesn't take away the misery of the illness, but the misery is bearable when Mum or Dad is there. Similarly, when we are suffering, God may not necessarily take the pain away for us, but he will comfort us with his presence. We can cope with the pain if we know that our heavenly Daddy is with us. It's as if God speaks to us by name, picks us up and cuddles us. We know that in the midst of our pain we are not isolated and alone; the Father is there with us, and he loves us.

Many Christians go through times of doubt and questioning. They wonder, 'Is Jesus really alive? Is my whole Christian faith just a trick I am playing on myself? Am I just imagining it all? Will I one day be able to die certain that Jesus really did take my sin and that beyond the grave there is eternal life for me?'

I don't know a single Christian of any worth who has never had a doubt. In those times of doubt, in those dark nights of the soul, Jesus longs to reach through the darkness into out hearts and speak to us by name: 'I'm alive. I love you. I'm not a figment of your imagination. I am not just a nice idea. I am real and I care about you.'

That was Mary's experience: Jesus was alive and he had reached out in love to her. We all need not only that baptism of love for Jesus which Mary had, but also this baptism of reality which she experienced. We all need to know the reality of the risen Christ; we need not only to believe that he is real but to know it in our hearts, to experience the risen Jesus for ourselves. We must all hear the voice of Jesus for ourselves, assuring us of his love for us, showing us how to live for him. We should not be satisfied with a superficial experience of Christ, or with drifting along in our Christian lives; we must hear God speaking to us personally, calling us by name as he did Mary. And when that happens, we are suddenly gripped by the immensity of eternity, and challenged by the Son of God. After that, we can never be the same again, because whatever arguments the world throws at us, we *know* that Jesus is alive and grips our being.

Jesus said (to Mary), '*Do not hold on to me, for I have not yet returned to the Father. Go instead to my brothers and tell them, "I am returning to my Father and your Father, to my God and your God."*'

Mary Magdalene went to the disciples with the news: 'I have seen the Lord!'

(John 20:17–18)

Mary had touched the risen Jesus. No-one could tell her that she had imagined it. All she had to say was, 'I've seen the Lord!' We can imagine something of the excitement she must have felt. We get excited when we experience Jesus, when we feel his presence, and when we see his power at work. And Mary had actually touched him. She had probably rushed up to him and hugged him, because she was so overjoyed to see him.

The Greek phrase which the NIV renders as *Do not hold on to me* ... is hard to translate, but I think the gist of it is that Jesus was saying to her, 'Wait a minute, Mary. I'm not going back to the Father just yet, so you'll have time to see me. I'll be around for a while longer yet. Right now I want you to go and tell the others that I'm alive, and then come back here to me, and then we'll talk.' And so she rushed off to tell the other disciples, 'Jesus is alive! I hugged him! I spoke to him! He's alive, I tell you!'

Jesus is no longer physically present on earth, because after he rose from death he ascended to heaven (see Acts 1). Today no-one can touch him physically as Mary did. But the Holy Spirit, whom Jesus had promised to send, and who came to the disciples after Jesus' ascension (see Acts 2), is with us today. Through him we can know and experience the risen Lord Jesus just as powerfully as Mary did. Countless Christians all over the world can testify that Jesus is alive today. They know he is living within them in the power of the Holy Spirit. Jesus lives with them day by day, talking to them, guiding them, filling their hearts with his love, giving them the power they need to serve him. This living Jesus longs to reach into all our lives and make us his own and call us by name.

Chapter 10

Thomas and Peter

Proof for a doubter

> On the evening of that first day of the week, when the
> disciples were together, with the doors locked for fear of the
> Jews, Jesus came and stood among them and said, 'Peace
> be with you!' After he said this, he showed them his hands
> and side. The disciples were overjoyed when they saw the
> Lord.
>
> (John 20:19–20)

Jesus had appeared to the disciples, and so they now
knew for themselves that Mary really had seen him.
They could see for themselves that God had done the
most wonderful miracle in history. Jesus had died that
terrible death on the cross, he had been in the tomb
for three days, and yet here he was, alive and talking to
them! They had scarcely dared to believe that what
Mary had reported to them could be true, and yet now
they had the evidence before their own eyes.

> Now Thomas (called Didymus), one of the Twelve, was not
> with the disciples when Jesus came. So the other disciples told
> him, 'We have seen the Lord!'
> But he said to them, 'Unless I see the nail marks in his
> hands and put my finger where the nails were, and put my
> hand into his side, I will not believe it.'
>
> (verses 24–25)

'Doubting Thomas' has gone down in history as a man

who lacked faith. It is true that his attitude showed a lack of faith in God and Jesus. He would not believe that Jesus had risen from death, even though Jesus himself had on a number of occasions promised that this would happen. Also, Thomas's attitude expressed a lack of faith in the reliability of the other disciples as witnesses. He doubted even though all the disciples were telling him that they had seen Jesus alive. In effect he was saying that they were all either liars or self-deluded fools.

But a week later Jesus appeared once more to the disciples and this time Thomas was with them. Jesus said to Thomas,

'Put your finger here; see my hands. Reach out your hand and put it into my side. Stop doubting and believe.'

(verse 27)

This is a very moving story. Even though Thomas had an unbelieving attitude, Jesus lovingly appeared to the disciples once more so that Thomas's doubts could be dispelled. Thomas was suitably humbled and convinced by this, and could say nothing to Jesus but

'My Lord and my God!'
    Then Jesus told him, 'Because you have seen me, you have believed; blessed are those who have not seen and yet have believed.'

(verses 28–29)

Thomas, despite all the wonderful things he had heard Jesus say and despite all the miracles he had seen him do, had needed Jesus to make a special post-resurrection appearance just to convince him that he really had risen from death. Jesus now praised all those people throughout the future history of the church who would never see the Lord in the flesh and yet would believe in him more readily than Thomas did.

Can we hear echoes of the story of Thomas in our

own lives? Perhaps we should not be too hasty to write him off as an unbelieving man. Maybe there is a little of the doubting Thomas in many of us. Perhaps part of Thomas's problem was a sort of 'spiritual jealousy'. Perhaps he was angry about the fact that Mary and the other disciples had all seen the risen Jesus, but he had not seen him. Probably through no fault of his own, it so happened that he was not there when Jesus had appeared. Maybe he felt rejected by this. He said to himself, 'Why is it that all the others have had this wonderful experience, but I haven't?'

Sometimes we can have a jealous attitude like that. We hear of wonderful things happening to other Christians, and really we would like God to do similar things for us. A feeling of resentment starts to smoulder in our hearts: 'Why does God always seem to do exciting things for other people and not for me? Why do I always seem to get left out?' And this resentment may lead us to say that we don't believe that the things which are happening to other Christians are genuine. 'If they're not happening in my life, why should they be happening in someone else's life? It's all probably wishful thinking and group hysteria!'

If that's our attitude, maybe Jesus will be gracious to us, as he was to Thomas, and will come and convince us of the reality of what he is doing, leaving us no room for doubts or criticism. But if we hear of wonderful things happening to other Christians – perhaps a spectacular physical healing or a powerful experience of the presence of God – and we are tempted to criticize it, what we need to do is to examine our own hearts. We need to ask ourselves, 'Why am I sceptical about this? Is what I'm hearing about really unlikely, bearing in mind the great love and power of Jesus? Why am I so negative? Is it because I would really like Jesus to do something like that for me, but I'm just jealous?'

What we need to do then is to put jealousy and

doubting and criticism aside and to ask Jesus to meet the deep desires of our hearts, and to come and work in us in love and depth and power. If we want Jesus to be real to us, let's not be jealous when he makes himself real to other people. Let's ask him with all our hearts to do the same for us too.

Hope for a backslider

Peter must have suffered a crushing sense of guilt during Jesus' trial and crucifixion. He had denied knowing Jesus three times. He had said he would stick with Jesus through thick and thin, but when it came to the crunch his courage failed him. He had not been willing to stand up and be identified with Jesus, because he didn't want to die. He probably felt he was a traitor to Jesus. We can imagine the desperate sense of failure and desolation he must have felt during those days while Jesus lay in the tomb. Peter must have hated himself for denying Jesus. He had thought he was a strong man, zealously committed to following Jesus, and yet once Jesus was arrested he had distanced himself from him to save his own skin.

And yet there was hope for Peter. On that never-to-be-forgotten morning, Mary had come running to him, telling him that Jesus' tomb was empty! Peter ran to the tomb and saw for himself that the body was indeed gone. What did it mean? Through the fog of his own shame and self-loathing, Peter may have dimly remembered Jesus' promises that he would rise from the dead.

Later in the day Mary excitedly reported that she had seen Jesus and spoken with him. And that evening Jesus had appeared to all of them (except Thomas). There could be no doubt that Jesus was alive! Peter was overjoyed, and yet … what did Jesus think of him now, after he had denied him, not just once, but three times? Mingled with Peter's joy there must have been some worry. Did Jesus still love him? After the terrible thing Peter had done, did Jesus still want him as his servant? Did all those things Jesus had said about Peter being a leader still hold true, or had Peter blown all that by his denial? Would Jesus choose someone else to lead his people, with Peter tagging along somewhere in the background on sufferance?

In John 21 we read that the risen Jesus appeared once more to the disciples by the Sea of Tiberias (or Galilee) while they were out fishing. They had caught nothing during the night, but

Early in the morning, Jesus stood on the shore, but the disciples did not realise that it was Jesus.

(verse 4)

He told them to throw the net in the water on the right side of the boat. They did as he told them, and

they were unable to haul the net in because of the large number of fish.

(verse 6)

They then realized that the man on the shore was Jesus.

I think this passage is telling us something about our work for Jesus – especially about evangelism, about 'catching' people and bringing them to know Jesus. It is crucial that we listen to his voice and that we do our work for him in the way in which he wants it to be done. We need to let down our nets precisely where he tells us to. If we wait for his prompting and guidance, rather than rushing off and doing what seems to us to be a good idea, our nets will be full. We will not waste our time and energy, and our work for Jesus, sooner or later, will be rewarded by ample results.

Verse 11 tells us that even though there were 153 large fish in the net, the net was not torn. Not one of the fish was lost. This tells us that Jesus takes the business of catching people very seriously. All of those people are precious to him, and he wants none of them to escape the net. If we witness about Jesus in the way he wants us to, our nets will not break and none of the people whom Jesus wants in his kingdom will get away.

Amazingly, the risen Jesus even cooked some of the fish for the disciples. After they had finished their meal, Jesus asked Peter three times whether he loved him. Each time Peter answered with a sincere 'Yes, of course, Lord!' Perhaps Jesus wanted Peter to say this three times in order to annul Peter's three denials of him.

In this conversation Jesus also gave Peter some orders to obey:

'Feed my lambs ... Take care of my sheep ... Feed my sheep ... Follow me!'

(verses 15–19)

Peter had reaffirmed his love for Jesus and his commitment to him. Jesus' response was to give him a job to do: to feed and take care of Jesus' people.

This tells us that although Peter had backslidden and had denied Jesus when the pressure was on, Jesus didn't reject him. Jesus knew that in his heart Peter loved him and wanted to serve him with his whole life. Jesus gave Peter a second chance. More than that, he reinstated Peter as the person who would lead his people once he had ascended to heaven. Peter had failed Jesus, but Jesus still wanted him on his team and gave him a crucially important job to do.

This story should be a great encouragement to Christians who think they have let Jesus down. Perhaps, like Peter, their commitment to Jesus cracked when the pressure became too intense, and when the cost of following Jesus seemed too high. And after the event they are left with a sense of guilt, failure and betrayal. They have turned away from Jesus, they have failed to obey him fully, they have backed away from full commitment to him, and now they wonder if Jesus will ever forgive them, and if he will ever want them back on his team again.

The story of Peter's denial tells us that Jesus is much kinder to us than we are to ourselves. We may have let him down, and we punish ourselves with the memory of it, with the shame of it. And yet Jesus says to us, 'Yes, you failed me, but I forgive you. Turn to me now and trust me, and let me do my work through you. You can still be a valued member of my team. Just turn back to me and depend on me for all the strength you will need.'

The fact that Peter was still the leader of Jesus' people, despite his denial of Jesus, should encourage Christian leaders today. We make mistakes and we sin, but if we come to God in total confession and repentance he will still use us. We do not lead by our own cleverness or giftedness, but by the grace of God. We are useless as leaders without his anointing. I know many leaders who feel unworthy to lead; they are acutely aware of their own failings and weaknesses. But if God reinstated Peter after his denial, there is hope for all of us. Feeling unworthy is the best state for a Christian leader to be in, because the alternative – arrogance – is ten times worse. Leaders who feel unworthy will be all the more likely to depend upon God for the ability to lead, whereas leaders who feel full of self-confidence will think they don't need God's strength to do the job.

Jesus is still at work today

John concludes his Gospel with the words,

Jesus did many other things as well. If every one of them were written down, I suppose that even the whole world would not have room for the books that would be written.

After his ascension into heaven and the sending of the Holy Spirit on the church, Jesus was able to work in countless people all over the world. John's words are true: Jesus has worked in so many millions of Christians throughout the centuries since the beginning of the church that if their testimonies about his power and love were all written down, not even all the libraries in the world would be able to contain them.

And today, there are countless millions of people all over the world, in every continent, who know Jesus personally, and who know what it is to have a relationship with him. Jesus is alive today, working in Christians in every nation. Perhaps when Jesus returns, we will somehow be able to grasp and understand the full scale of what he has done in people through the centuries. And it is certain that the sum of what he has done will be far, far greater than anything we can imagine.